# MECHANICAL ENGINEERING DIPLOMA & ENGINEERING MCQ

MANOJ DOLE

Made with ♥ on the Notion Press Platform
www.notionpress.com

**Mechanical Engineering Diploma & Engineering MCQ** is a simple Book for Mechanical Diploma & Engineering Course, It contains objective questions with underlined & bold correct answers MCQ covering all topics including all about the latest & Important about Engineering Physics, Applied Mechanics, Engineering Drawing/Graphics, Material Science, Mechanical Drafting, Communication Skills, Basic Civil Engineering, Manufacturing Engineering, Fluid Mechanics, Thermal Engineering, Thermodynamics, Theory of Machines, Strength of Materials, CADD, Applied Electronics and Electrical Engineering, Metrology and Instrumentation, CADD (Computer Aided Machine Design and Drawing), Plant Maintenance and Safety, Thermal Engineering, Computer Aided Manufacturing, Design of Machine Elements, Tool Engineering, Manufacturing Engineering, Industrial Manufacturing, Industrial Design and lots more.

We add new question answers with each new version. Please email us in case of any errors/omissions. This is arguably the largest and best Book for All engineering multiple choice questions and answers.

As a student you can use it for your exam prep. This Book is also useful for professors to refresh material.

# Contents

# Foreword

This book may be purchased for educational, business, or sales promotional use. Online edition is also available for this title. For more information, contact our corporate/institutional sales department: [manojdole1@gmail.com]

While every precaution has been taken in the preparation of this book, the publisher and authors assume no responsibility for errors or omissions, or for damages resulting from the use of the information contained herein.

**About the Author**

MANOJ DOLE is an Engineer from reputed University. He is currently working with Government Industrial Training- Institute as a lecturer from last 12 Years. His interest include- Engineering Training Material, Invention & Engineering Practical- Knowledge etc.

CHAPTER ONE

# Mechanical Engineering Hand Tools & Measuring Instruments Theory

Download App
Online Test Exam
ITI Books
AutoCAD CAM
JOB & Apprentice
Online Theory
Computer Course
Trading Course
CNC Course
MSCIT Course
Shopping Business
Internet Business
Web Designing
Online Services
Top Sportsmans
Indian Army
Freedom Fighters
Top Scientists
Social Reformers
Motivational Speaker
Top Richest People
Join WhatsApp Group
Join Facebook Group
Like Facebook Page
PAN / Adhar / Licence
Passport

Fire extinguisher

Calliper

Hacksaw frame

Universal surface guage

Hammer

Centre punch

Bench vice

Files

Scraper

Surface Plate

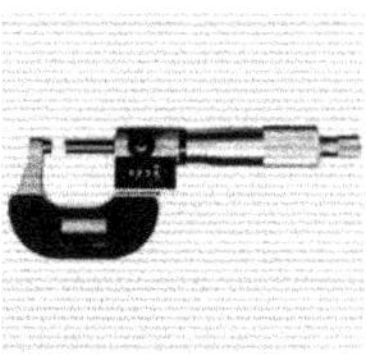

Outside Micrometer

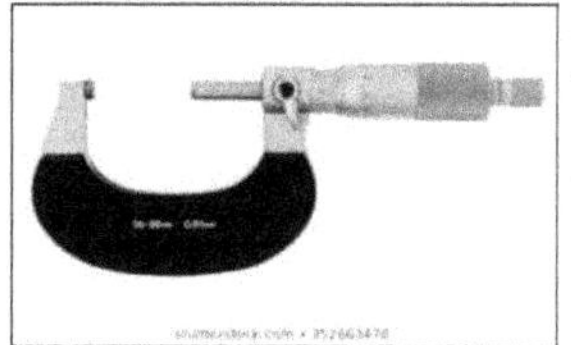

Micrometer

Depth micrometer

Vernier Calliper

Vernier bevel protractor

Drilling

Reamer

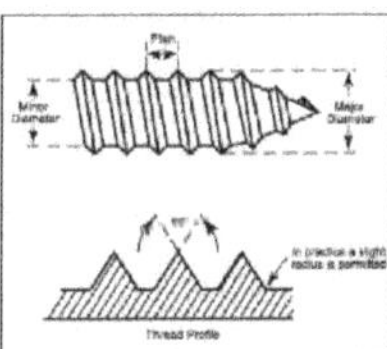

Thread

Tap Die

Grinding Wheel

Slip gauge

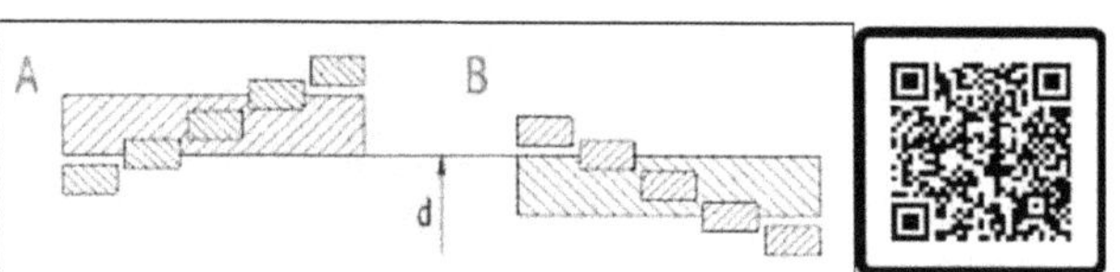


Limit fit tolerance

Lathe Machine

Lathe chuck

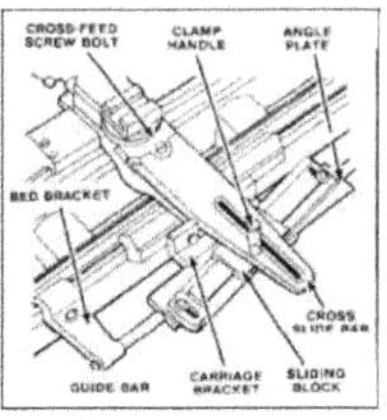

Taper turning attachment

taper ring gauge

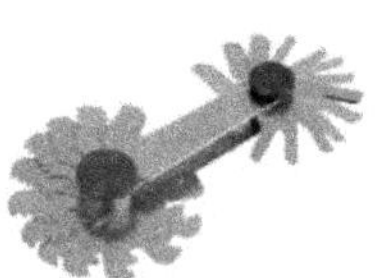

screw pitch gauge

Gear

screw pitch gauge

Tap Die

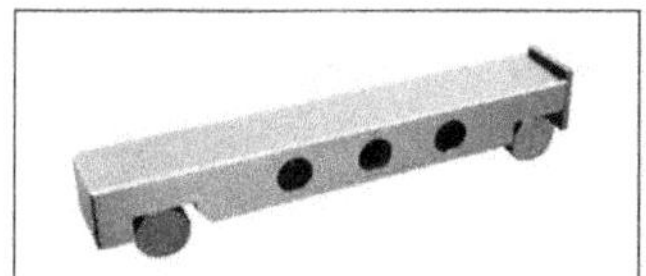

Sine bar

Slip gauge

Dial test indicator

Telescopic gauge

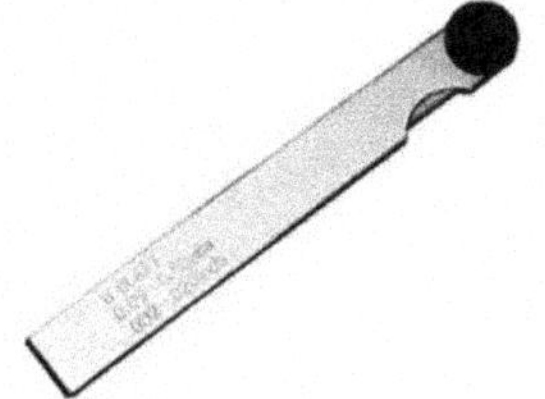

Feeler gauge

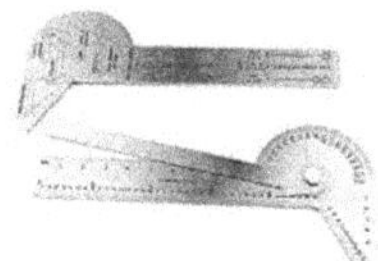

Centre gauge

Jig

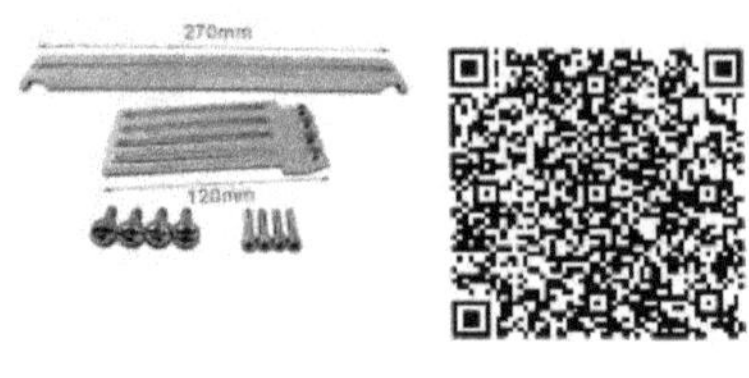

Fixture

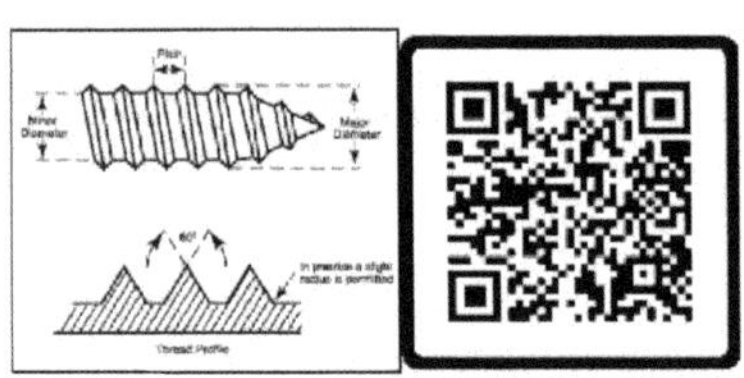

Thread

CHAPTER TWO

# Mechanical Engineering Machines Theory

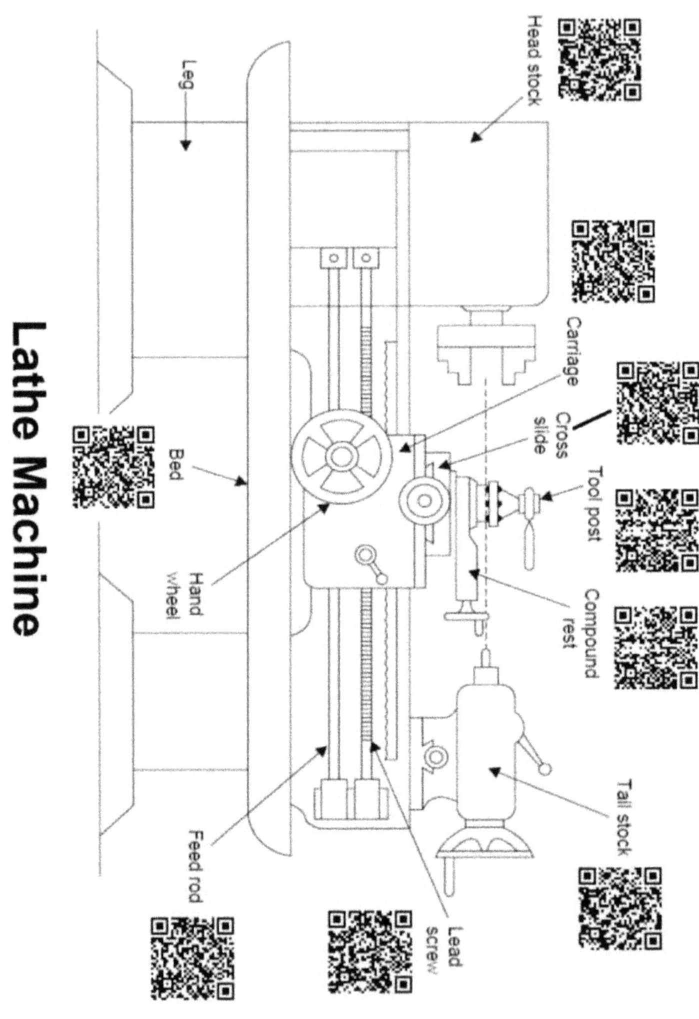
Lathe Machine
Head stock
Leg
Carriage
Cross slide
Tool post
Compound rest
Bed
Hand wheel
Tail stock
Feed rod
Lead screw

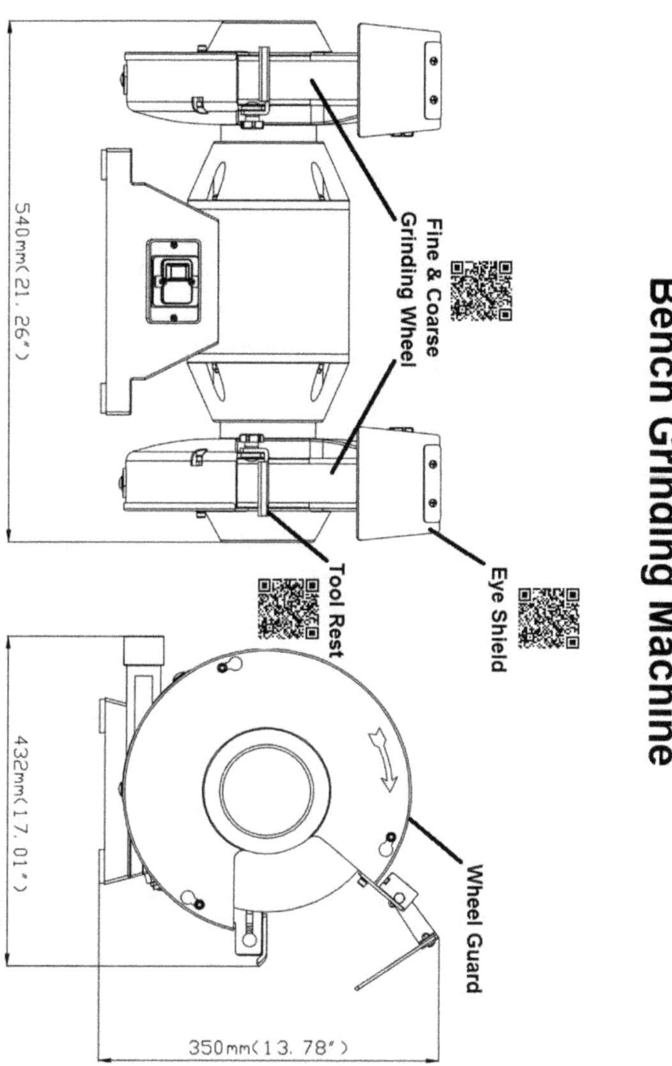
Bench Grinding Machine
Fine & Coarse
Grinding Wheel
Eye Shield
Tool Rest
Wheel Guard
540mm(21.26")
432mm(17.01")
350mm(13.78")

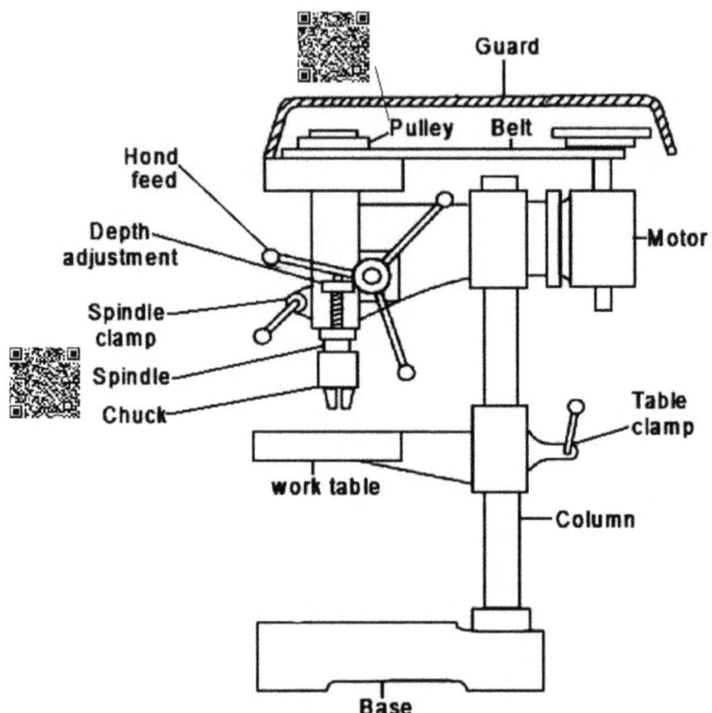


# Piller Drilling Machine

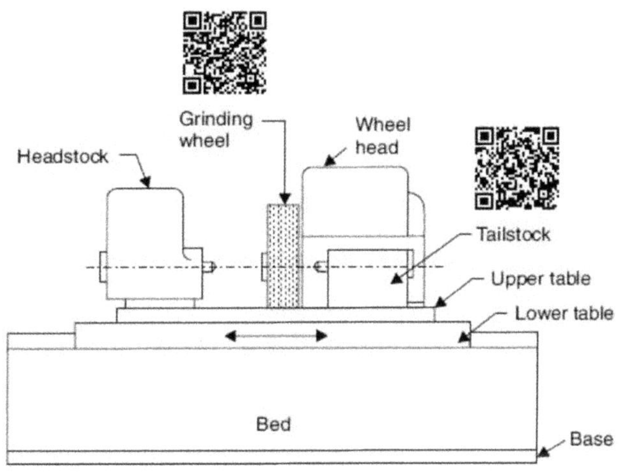


plain cylindrical grinder

Work head motor
Wheel head motor
Grinding wheel
Work
table
Head stock
centre
Tail
stock
Reversing
trips
Table hand
control
Wheel feed
control
Base
Control pannel

**Cylindrical grinding machine**

To study Different operations and parts of Surface Grinding Machine

# SURFACE GRINDER

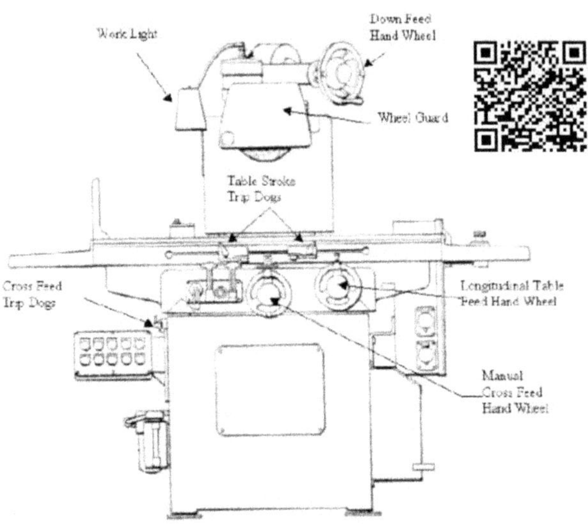


**Surface grinding is used to produce a smooth finish on flat surfaces. It is a widely used abrasive machining process in which a spinning wheel covered in rough particles (grinding wheel) cuts**

# PLAIN OR HORIZONTAL MILLING MACHINE

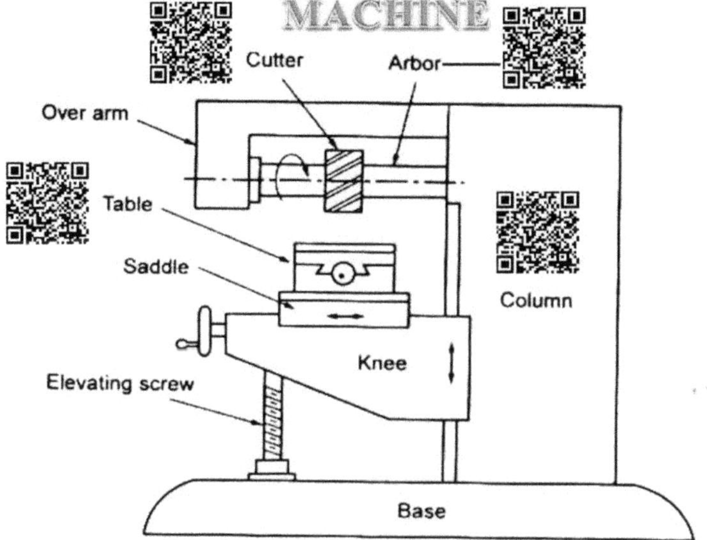

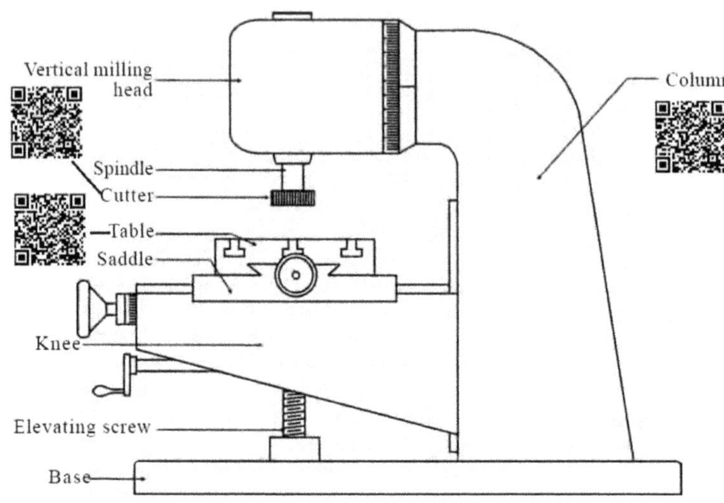


**Vertical Milling Machine**

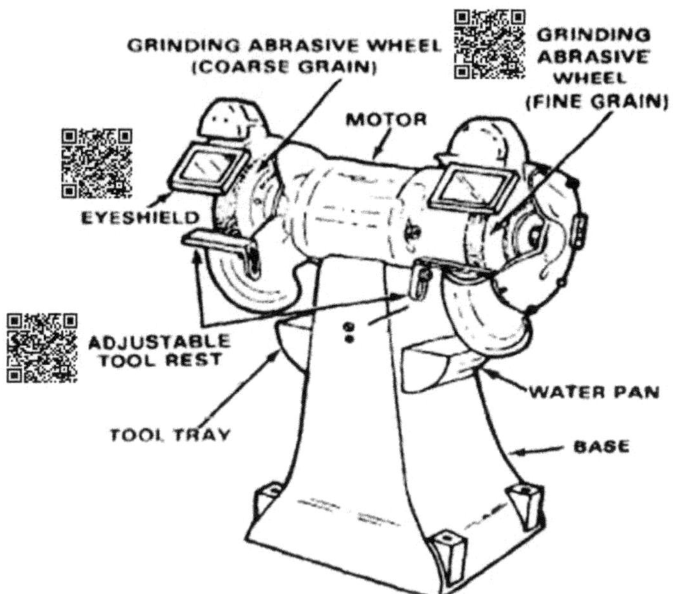


**Pedastal Grinding Machine**

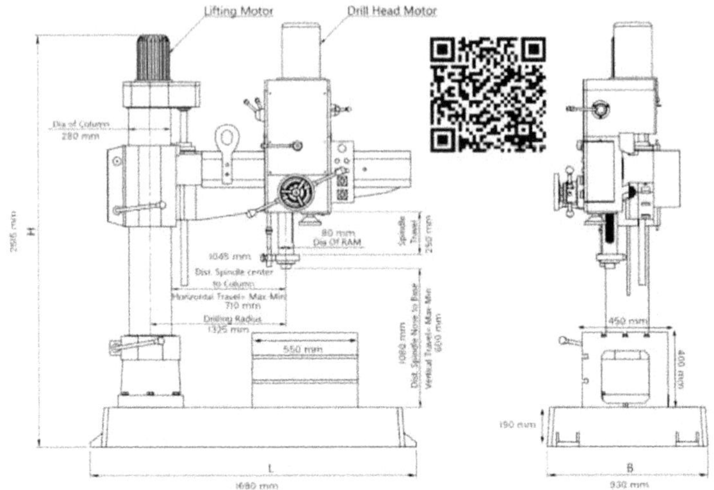


**Radial Drilling Machine**

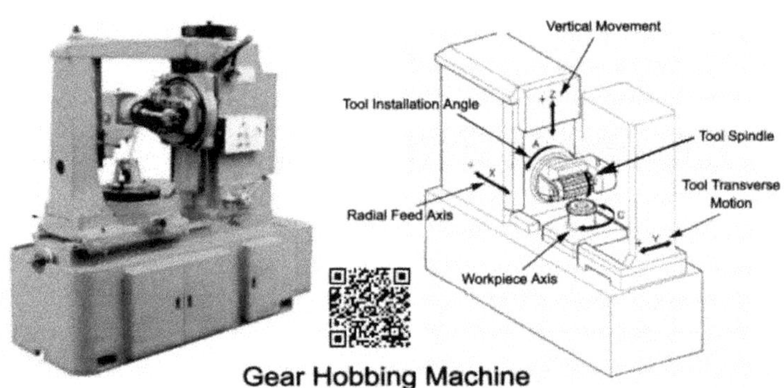


**Gear Hobbing Machine**

# DOUBLE HOUSING PLANER

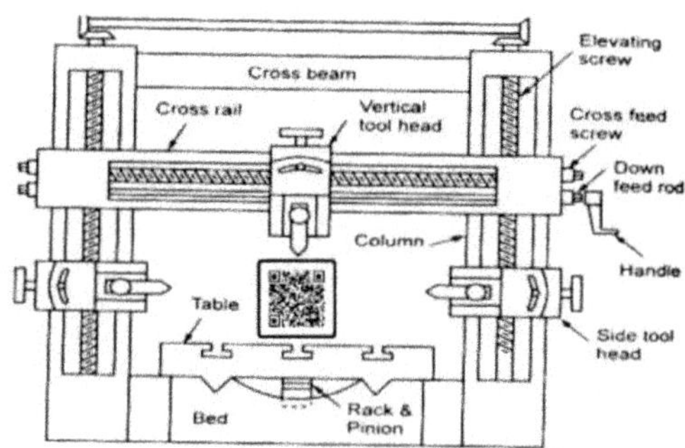


# PIT PLANER

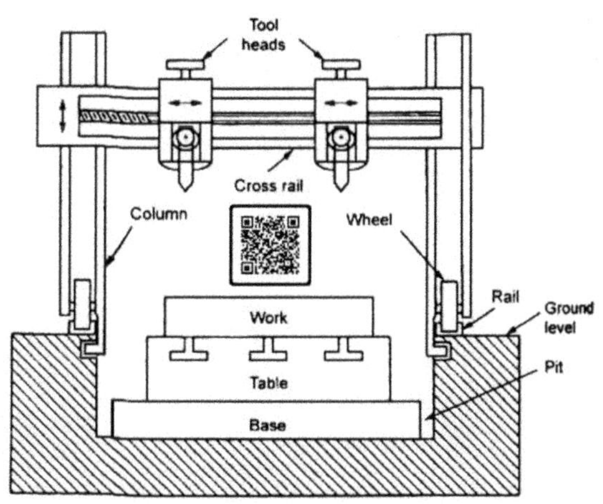

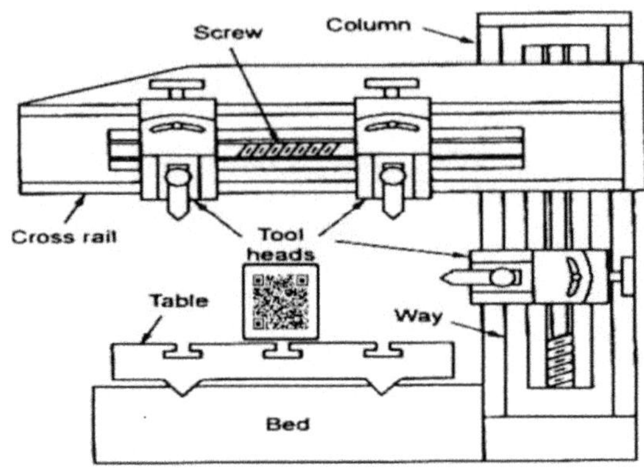


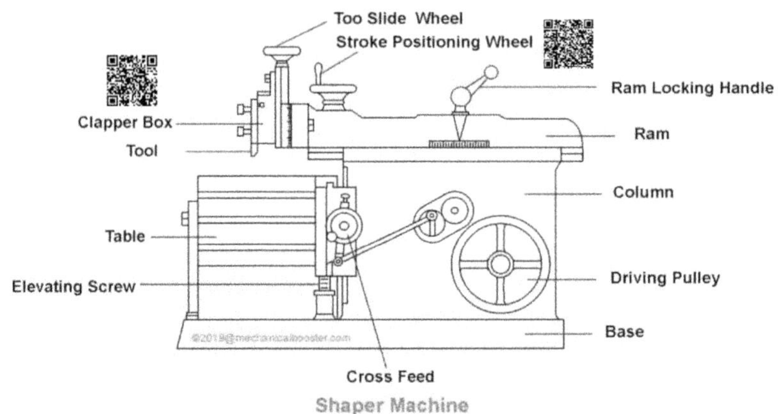


Shaper Machine

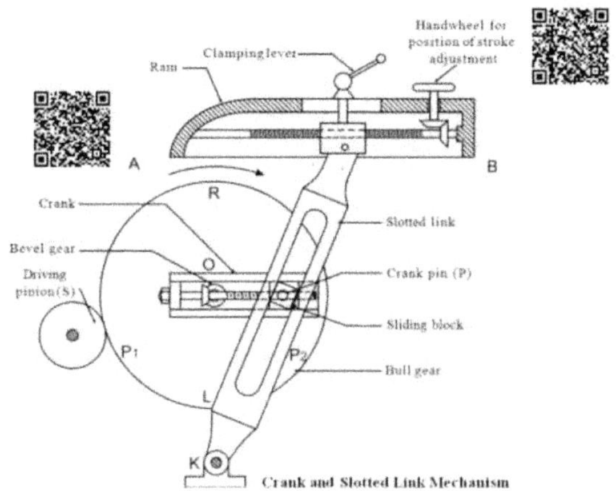


**Quick Return Mechanism of Shaper Machine**

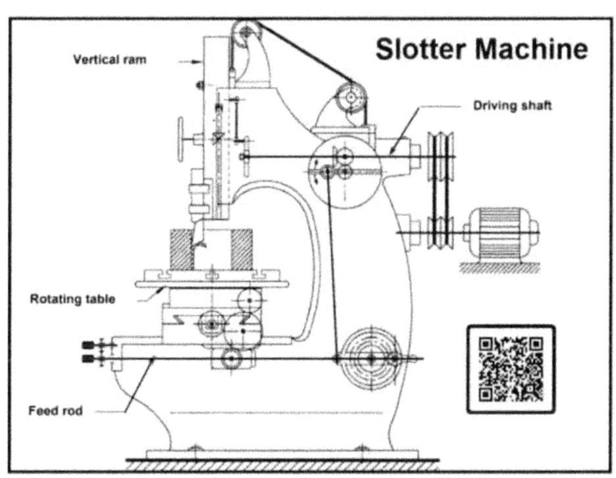

CHAPTER THREE

# Mechanical Engineering Drawing Theory

Grinding

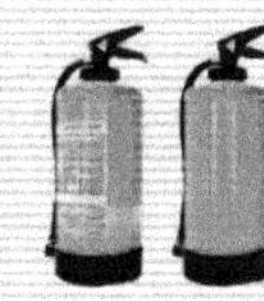

Fire extinguisher

French curve in drawing

Set square in drawing

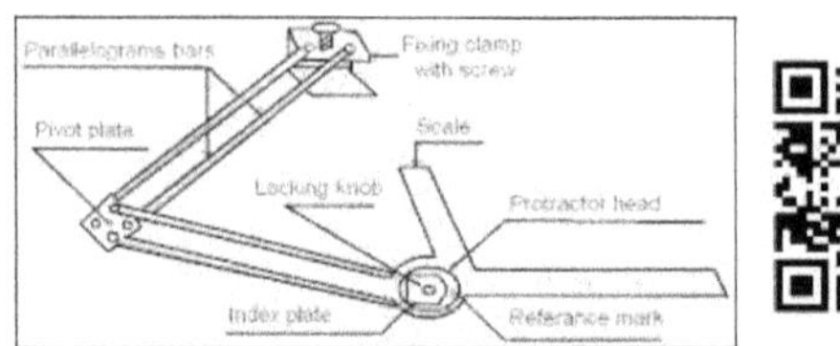


Mini drafter in drawing

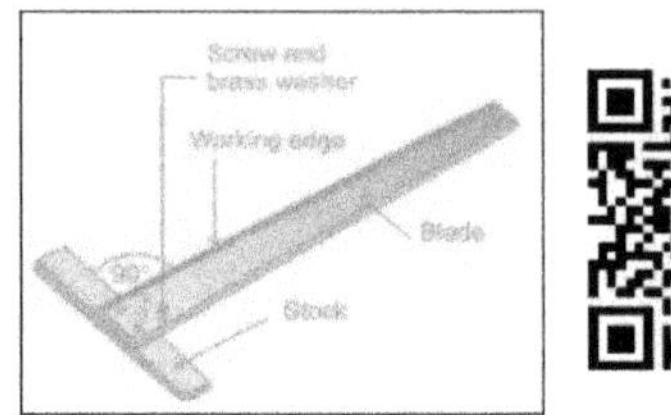

T - square in drawing

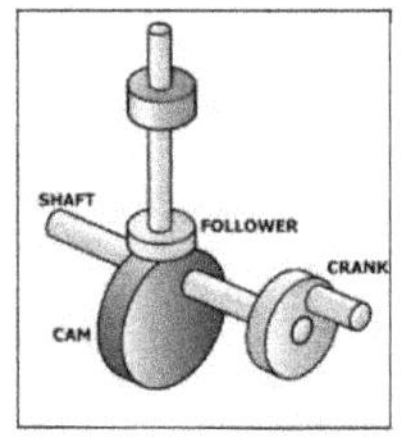

Cams in engine

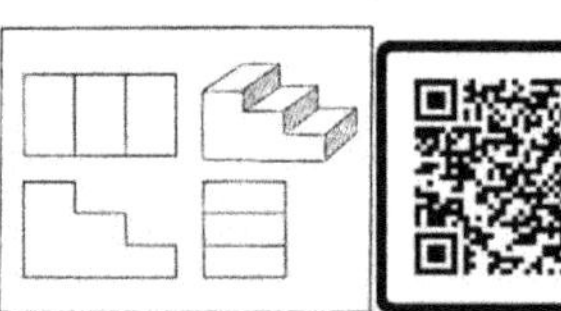

Orthographic projection in drawing

Third angle projection drawing

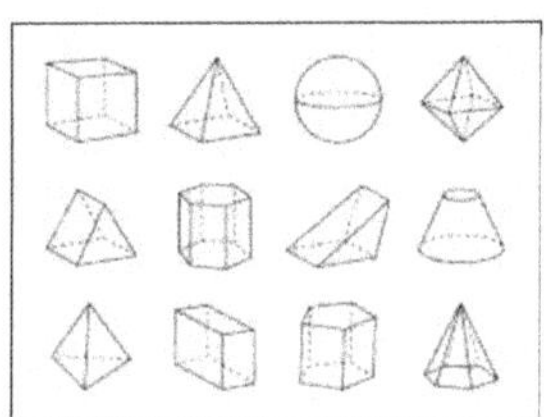

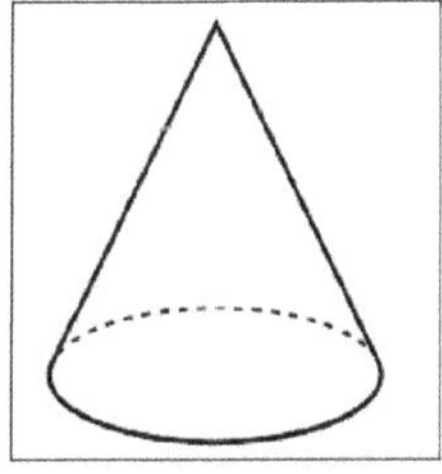

Cone in engineering drawing

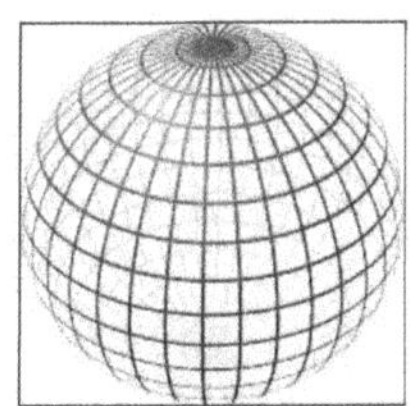

Sphere in drawing

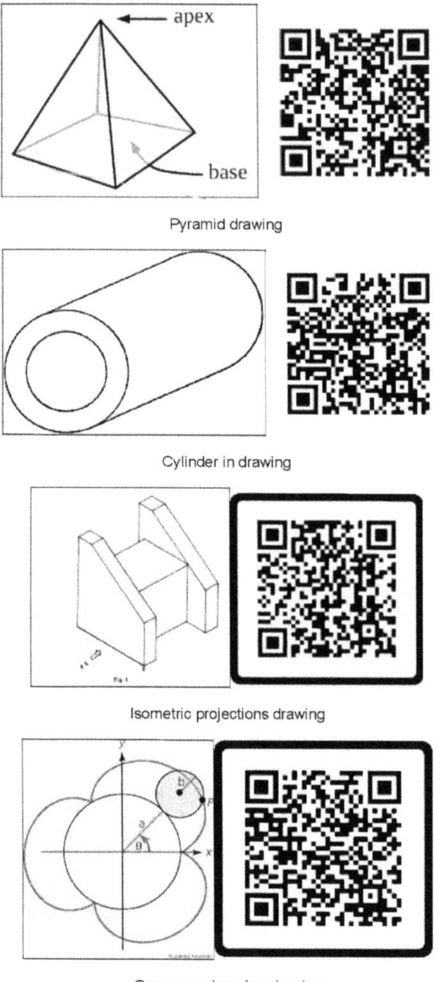


Pyramid drawing

Cylinder in drawing

Isometric projections drawing

Curves engineering drawing

Sectional views in drawing

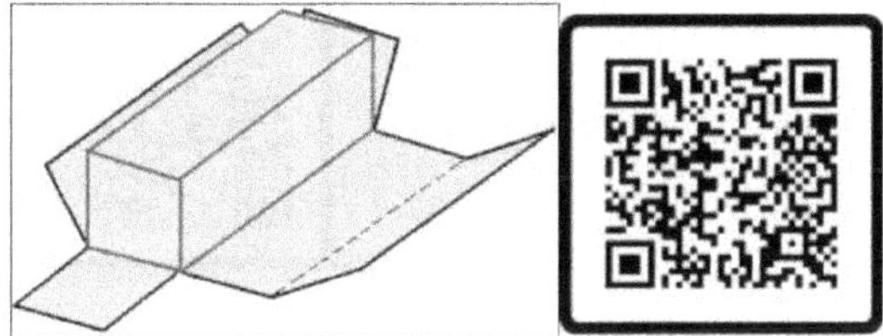

Development of surfaces in drawing

Hexagonal plane in drawing

Polyhedron in drawing

First Angle projection method in drawing

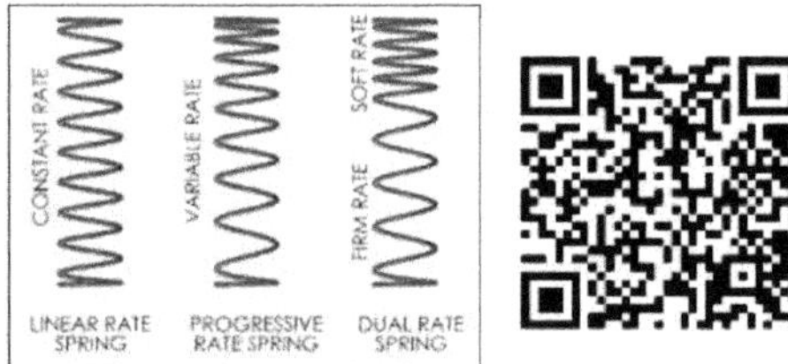


Springs in drawing

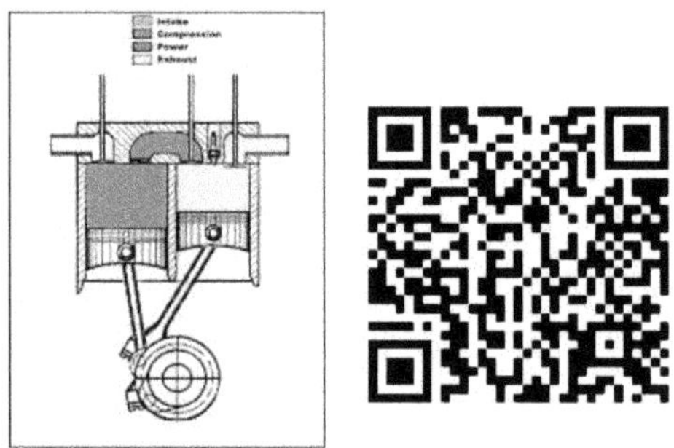

Engine in vehicle

CHAPTER FOUR

# Mechanical Engineering AutoCAD Theory

## AutoCAD Command Shortcut Keys

| | |
|---|---|
| CTRL+Q | Exit public consciousness |
| CTRL+R | Remove ornamentation |
| CTRL+S | Save as Stainless Steel |
| CTRL+SHFT+S | Save as a better design (ie. Titanium) |
| CTRL+T | Toggles Talent (requires administrative access) |
| CTRL+V | Value Engineer (reduces scale by 78%) |
| CTRL+SHFT+V | Pastes data from ArchRecord as Block |
| CTRL+X | Begin unpaid Furlough |
| CTRL+Y | Repeats last award winning design |
| CTRL+Z | Speed dial Zaha Hadid |
| CTRL+ZZZ | Sleep (not applicable) |
| CTRL+[ | Cancels current schedule |
| CTRL+\ | Cancels current budget |
| CTRL+ANGST+DEL | (no action) |

| | |
|---|---|
| F1 | Displays Help wanted sign in café window |
| F2 | Toggles all text to Helvetica |
| F3 | Toggles Oh-SNAP |
| F4 | Toggles MODERNISM |
| F5 | Toggles ISOLATION |
| F6 | Toggles CORBUSIER |
| F7 | Toggles IRRELEVANT GRID |
| F8 | Toggles ORTHO MODE (should always be on) |
| F9 | Toggles POSTMODERNISM (should always be off) |
| F10 | Toggles NORWAY |
| F11 | Toggles ARROGANCE |

## AutoCAD Command Shortcut Keys

| | |
|---|---|
| ALT+F8 | Delete detail |
| ALT+F11 | Add white |
| CTRL+1 | Simplify Palette |
| CTRL+2 | Remove Interior Design Palette |
| CTRL+3 | Complicate Construction Process |
| CTRL+4 | Add 4 extraneous sheets |
| CTRL+5 | Remove Client's color Palette |
| CTRL+6 | Remove Client's wife's color Palette (must press hard) |
| CTRL+7 | Markup Set for interns (with only circles and question marks) |
| CTRL+A | Selects objects in drawing that aren't really needed |
| CTRL+B | Sends resume to B.I.G. |
| CTRL+SHIFT+B | Shifts blame to Consultants |
| CTRL+C | Copies angst to Clipboard |
| CTRL+SHFT+C | Copies angst to Clipboard with Base Point (ie. Finland) |
| CTRL+D | Delete relevance |
| CTRL+E | Cycles through design ideologies |
| CTRL+F | Flatten all roofs |
| CTRL+G | Insert 9-square Grid |
| CTRL+H | Insert Awesomeness |
| CTRL+L | Adds "Le" in front of all nouns |
| CTRL+K | Justify design concept |
| CTRL+L | Left justify design concept |
| CTRL+M | Less and/or more |
| CTRL+N | Insert new idea (bills client for additional time required) |
| CTRL+O | Opens ArchDaily.com |
| CTRL+P | Prints unemployment check |

| Button | Command | Draw Panel |
|---|---|---|
| | LINE (L) | Line |
| | RAY | Ray (on slideout) |
| | XLINE (XL) | Construction Line (on slideout) |
| | PLINE (PL) | Polyline |
| | RECTANG (REC) | Rectangle |
| | POLYGON (POL) | Polygon (on the Rectangle drop-down menu) |

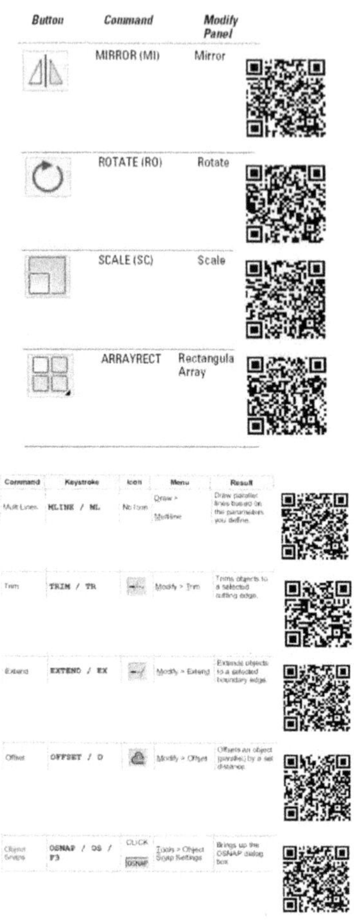

| Button | Command | Modify Panel |
|---|---|---|
| | MIRROR (MI) | Mirror |
| | ROTATE (RO) | Rotate |
| | SCALE (SC) | Scale |
| | ARRAYRECT | Rectangula Array |

| Command | Keystroke | Icon | Menu | Result |
|---|---|---|---|---|
| Mult Lines | MLINE / ML | No Icon | Draw > Multline | Draw parallel lines based on the parameters you define. |
| Trim | TRIM / TR | | Modify > Trim | Trims objects to a selected cutting edge. |
| Extend | EXTEND / EX | | Modify > Extend | Extends objects to a selected boundary edge. |
| Offset | OFFSET / O | | Modify > Offset | Offsets an object (parallel) by a set distance. |
| Object Snaps | OSNAP / OS / F3 | CLICK OSNAP | Tools > Object Snap Settings | Brings up the OSNAP dialog box |

| | | |
|---|---|---|
| | EXTEND (EX) | Extend (on drop-down button) |
| | LENGTHEN (LEN) | Lengthen (on slideout panel) |
| | BREAK (BR): two points | Break (on slideout panel) |
| | BREAK (BR): 1 point | Break at point (on slideout panel) |
| | EXPLODE (X) | Explode |
| | FILLET (F) | Fillet (on drop-down button) |

| Command | [illegible] | Icon | Menu | Result |
|---|---|---|---|---|
| Line | Line / L | | Draw > Line | Draws a straight line segment from one point to the next |
| Circle | Circle / C | | Draw > Circle > Center, Radius | Draws a circle based on a center point and radius |
| Erase | Erase / E | | Modify > Erase | Erases an object |
| Print | Print / Plot Cntl+P | | File > [illegible] | Enables the Print/Plot Configuration Dialog Box |
| Undo | U (Don't use Undo for now) | | Edit > Undo | Undoes the last command |
| Rectangle | RECTANGLE / REC | | Draw > Rectangle | Draws a rectangle after you enter one corner and then the second |

| Button | Command | Modify Panel |
| --- | --- | --- |
| | ERASE (E) | Erase |
| | MOVE (M) | Move |
| | COPY (CO or CP) | Copy |
| | STRETCH (S) | Stretch |
| | ARRAYPOLAR | Polar Array |
| | ARRAYPATH | Path Array |
| | ARRAYEDIT | Edit Array (on slideout panel) |
| | OFFSET (O) | Offset |
| | TRIM (TR) | Trim (on drop-down button) |

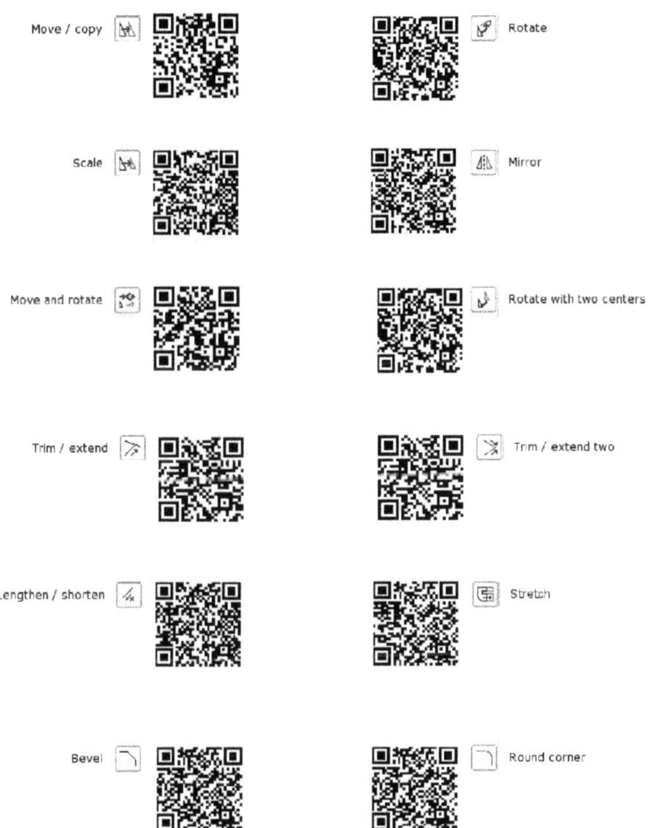
Move / copy
Rotate
Scale
Mirror
Move and rotate
Rotate with two centers
Trim / extend
Trim / extend two
Lengthen / shorten
Stretch
Bevel
Round corner

CHAPTER FIVE

# Mechanical Engineering Electrical Theory

14 ITI Book MCQ - Manoj Dole
www.itibook.com
battery
capacitor
cell
dynamometer
electromagnet
heater
inductance
magnet
www.itigov.blogspot.com www.jobapprentices.blogspot.com www.ititests.blogspot.com
www.itibook.com

15 ITI Book MCQ - Manoj Dole
www.itibook.com
megger
motor
multimeter
ohmmeter
resistores
star connected alternator
voltmeter
ammeter
wattmeter
www.itigov.blogspot.com www.jobapprentices.blogspot.com www.ititests.blogspot.com
www.itibook.com

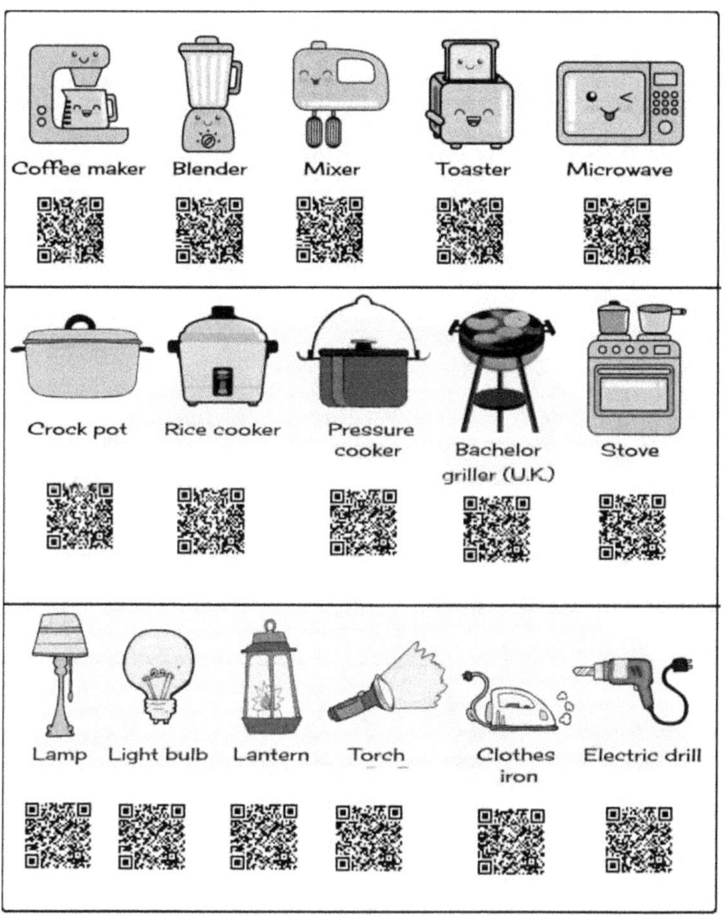
Coffee maker
Blender
Mixer
Toaster
Microwave
Crock pot
Rice cooker
Pressure cooker
Bachelor griller (U.K.)
Stove
Lamp
Light bulb
Lantern
Torch
Clothes iron
Electric drill

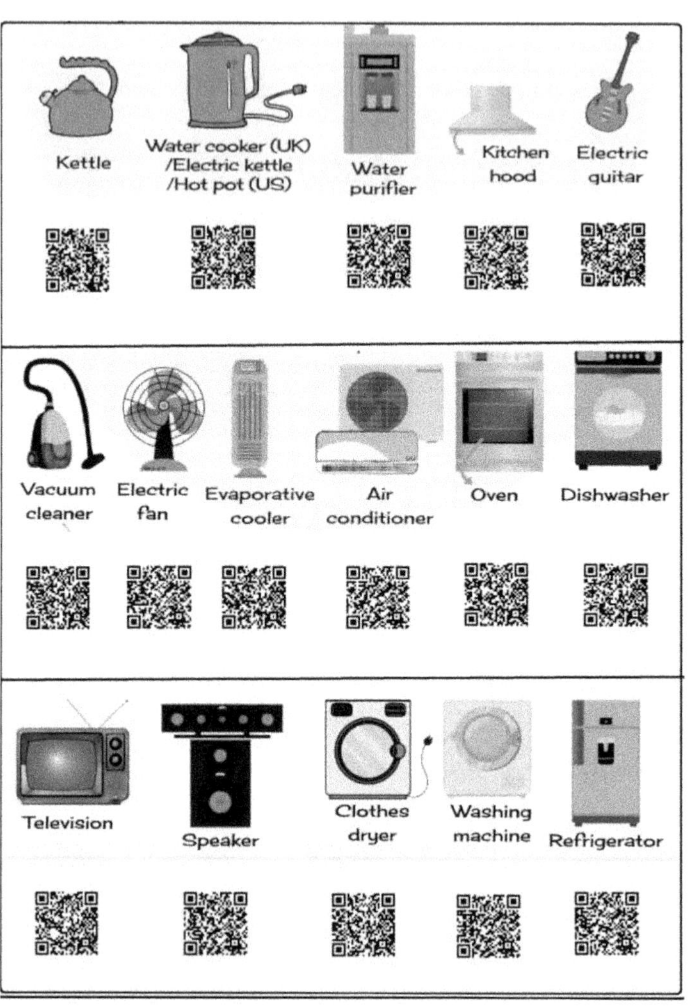
Kettle
Water cooker (UK)
/Electric kettle
/Hot pot (US)
Water
purifier
Kitchen
hood
Electric
guitar
Vacuum
cleaner
Electric
fan
Evaporative
cooler
Air
conditioner
Oven
Dishwasher
Television
Speaker
Clothes
dryer
Washing
machine
Refrigerator

CHAPTER SIX

# Mechanical Engineering CNC Machine Theory

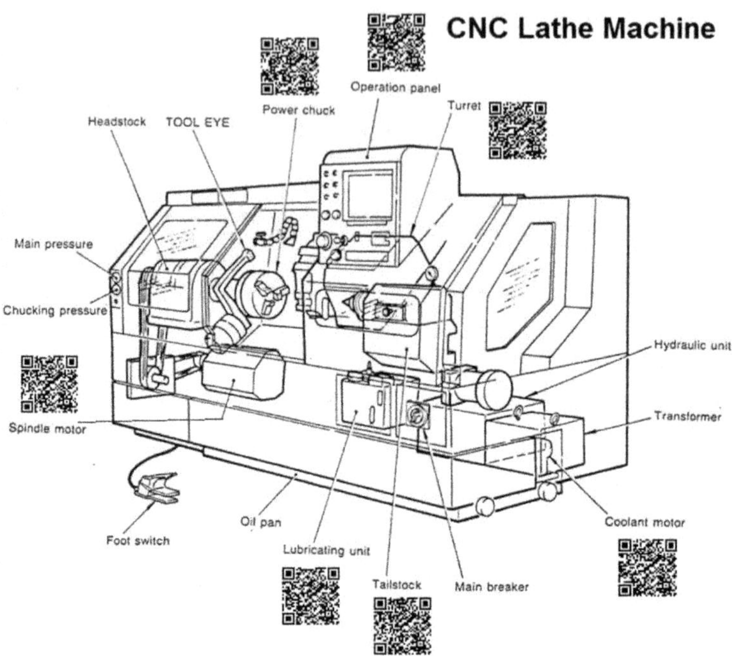
CNC Lathe Machine
Operation panel
Power chuck
Turret
Headstock
TOOL EYE
Main pressure
Chucking pressure
Hydraulic unit
Transformer
Spindle motor
Coolant motor
Oil pan
Foot switch
Lubricating unit
Tailstock
Main breaker

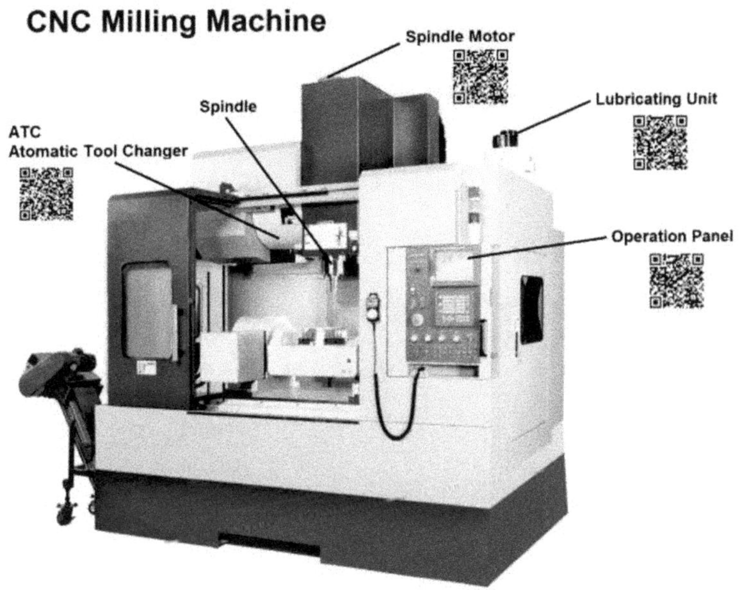


CNC Machine Lubrication

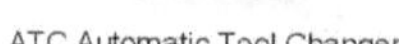

ATC Automatic Tool Changer

Animation & Video

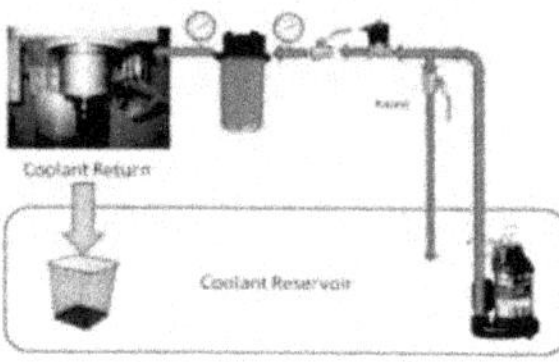

CNC Coolant Pump

Animation & Video

CHAPTER SEVEN

# Mechanical Engineering Welding Theory

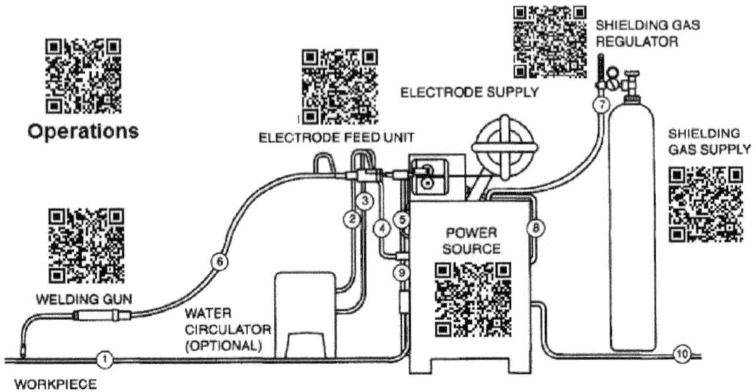


Gas Metal Arc Welding

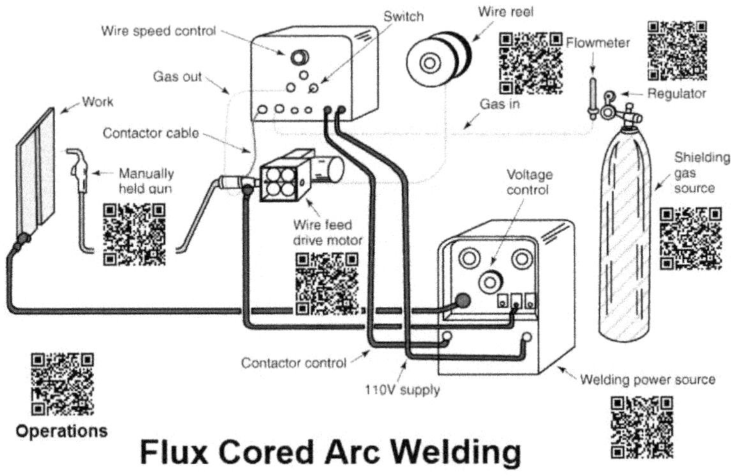


Flux Cored Arc Welding

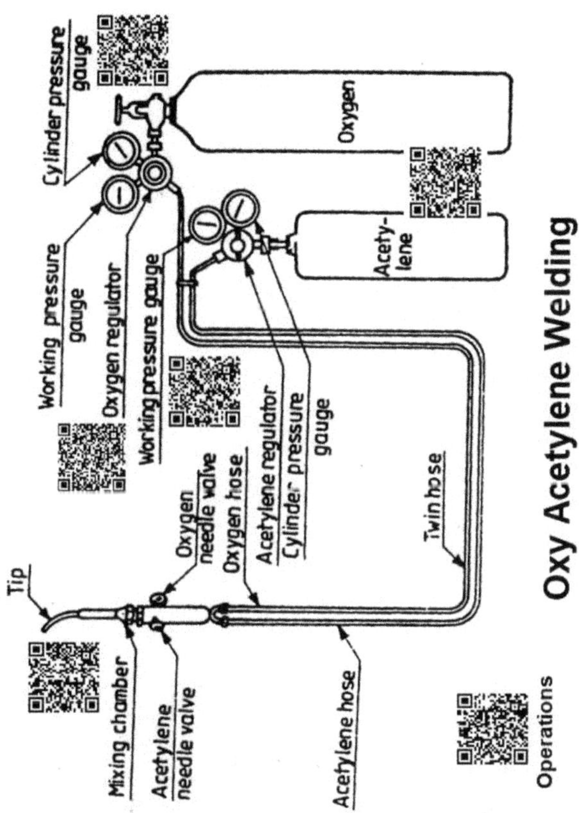
Cylinder pressure gauge
Working pressure gauge
Oxygen regulator
Working pressure gauge
Oxygen
Acety-lene
Acetylene regulator
Cylinder pressure gauge
Twin hose
Oxygen needle valve
Oxygen hose
Tip
Mixing chamber
Acetylene needle valve
Acetylene hose
Operations
Oxy Acetylene Welding

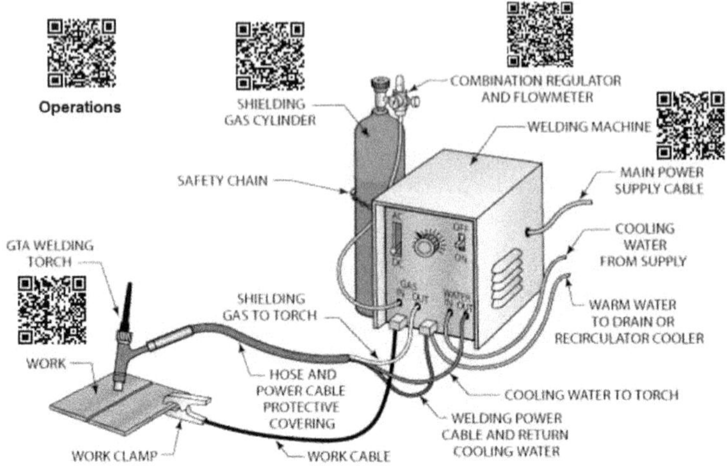


**GTAW EQUIPMENT**

**(GAS TUNGSTEN ARC WELDING)**

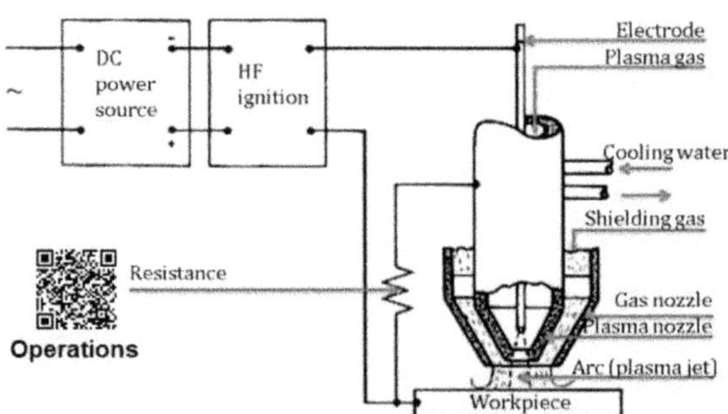


**Plasma Transferred Arc Welding**

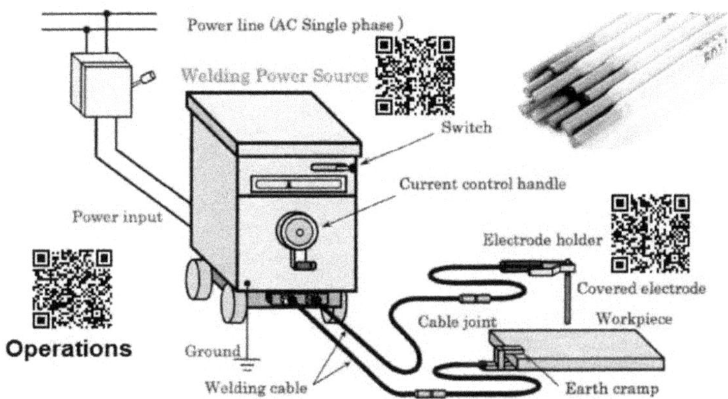


**Shielded Metal Arc Welding**

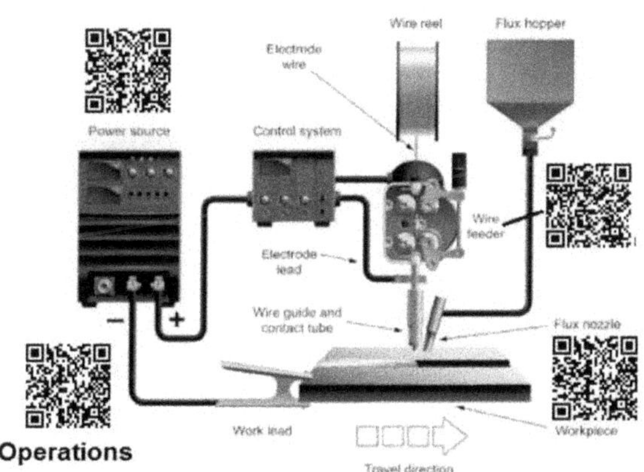


**Submerged Arc Welding**

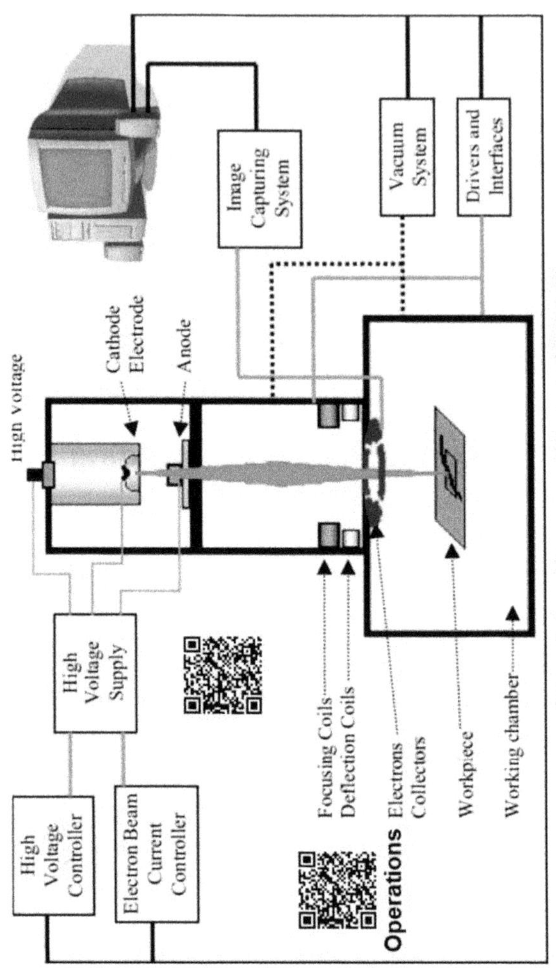
High Voltage
Cathode Electrode
Anode
Image Capturing System
Vacuum System
Drivers and Interfaces
High Voltage Supply
High Voltage Controller
Electron Beam Current Controller
Focusing Coils
Deflection Coils
Electrons Collectors
Workpiece
Working chamber
Operations
Electron Energy Beam Welding

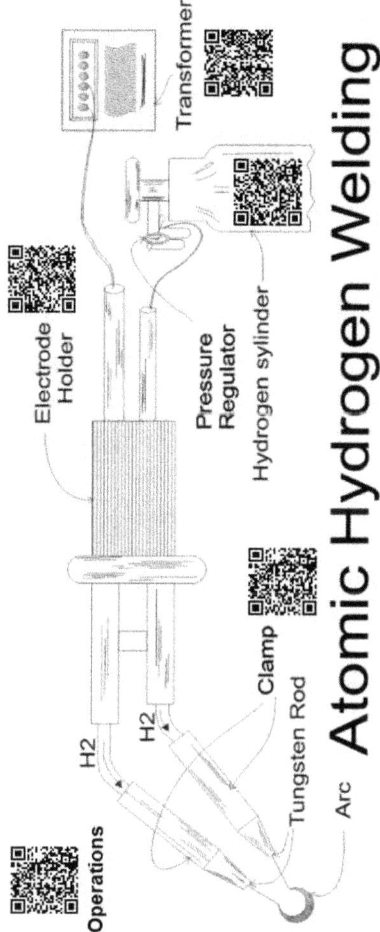
Atomic Hydrogen Welding
Transformer
Electrode
Holder
Pressure
Regulator
Hydrogen sylinder
Clamp
H2
H2
Tungsten Rod
Arc
Operations

nibbling machine

slant notch

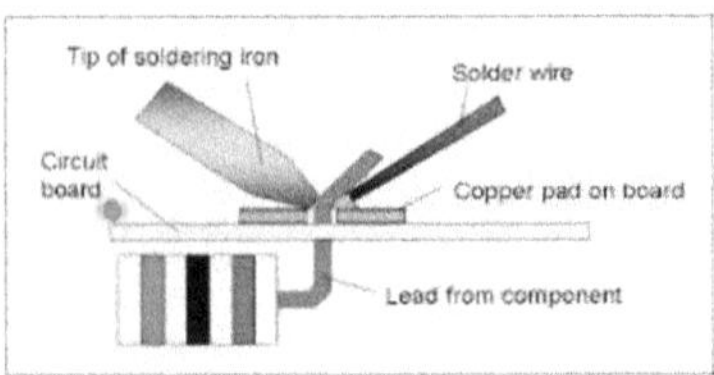

soldering

acytiline gas purifier

hydraulic back pressure valve

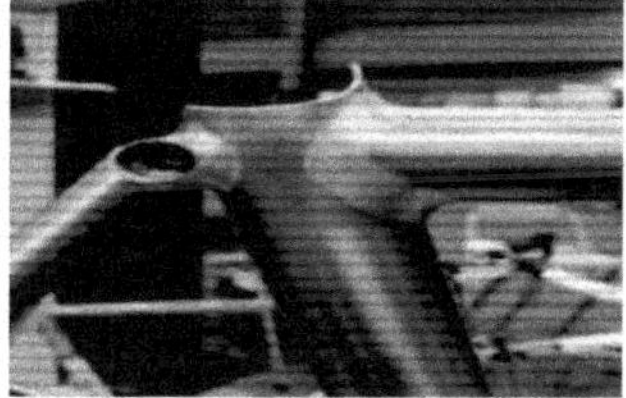

bronze welding

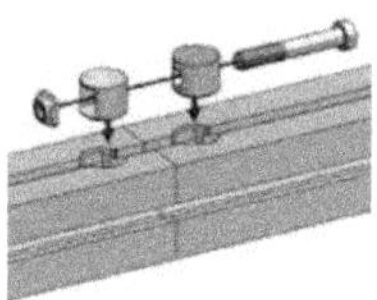

aluminium butt joint

coated electrodes

dc welding generator

nick break test

pipe welding

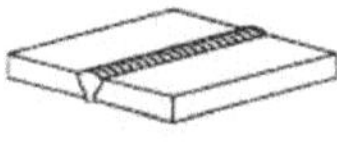

The butt weld

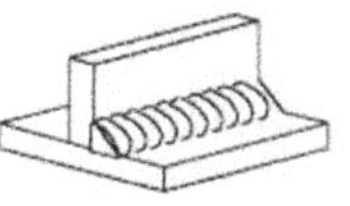

The fillet weld

Figure 1 The two basic types of weld

welding joints

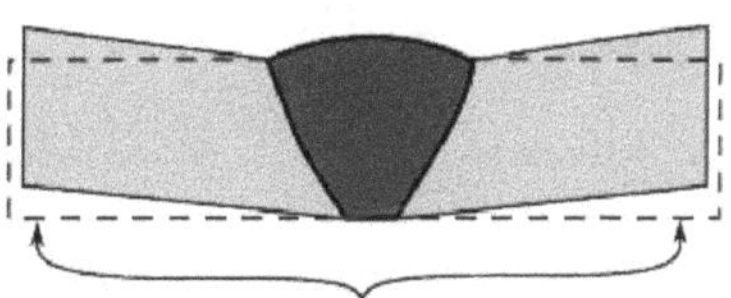

distortion

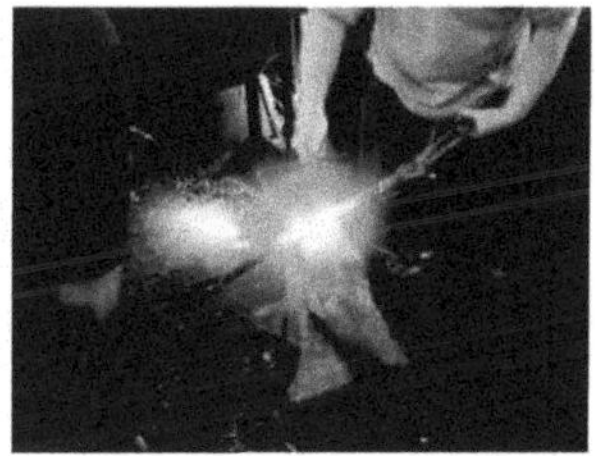

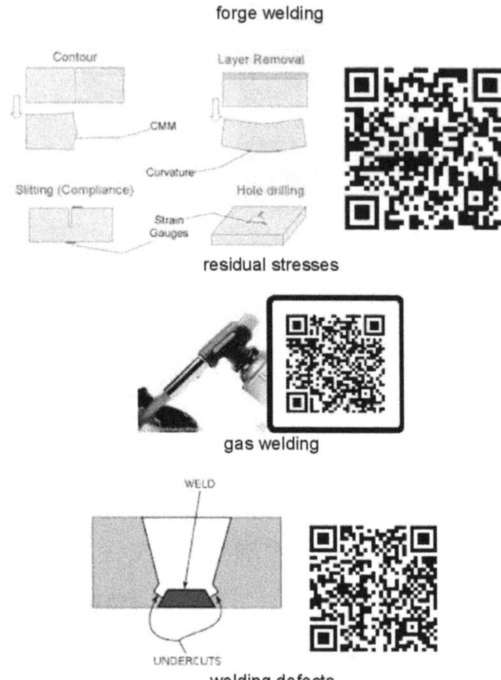


forge welding

residual stresses

gas welding

welding defects

CHAPTER EIGHT

# Mechanical Engineering Computer Skill Theory

COMPUTER PARTS
COMPUTER
MOUSE
KEY BOARD
SCREEN / MONITOR
FLASH DRIVE
TOWER
COMPACT DISC
LAPTOP
PRINTER
SCANNER
CARTRIDGES
WEB CAM

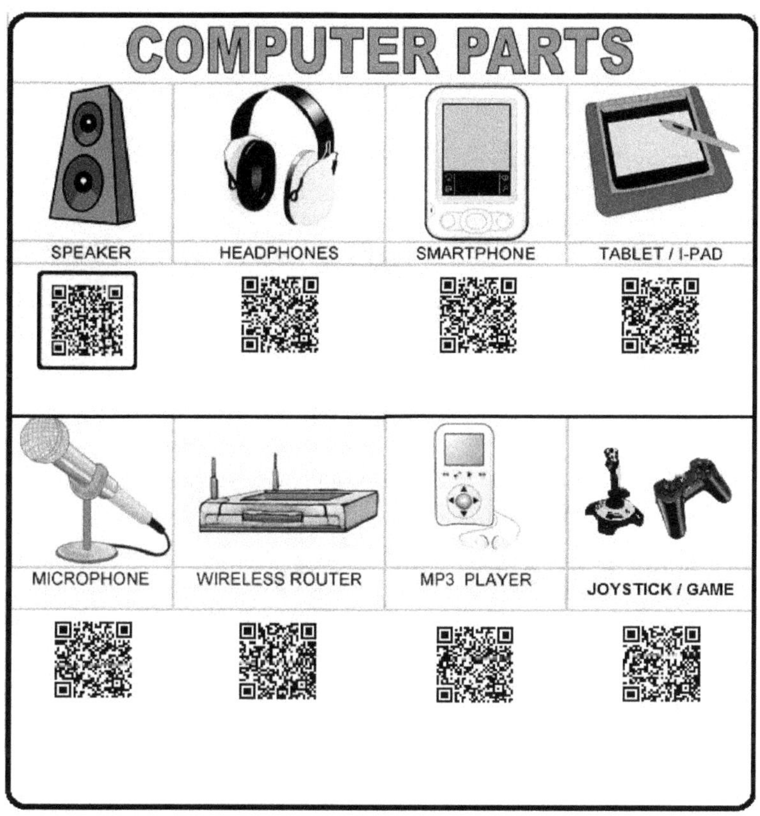
COMPUTER PARTS
SPEAKER
HEADPHONES
SMARTPHONE
TABLET / I-PAD
MICROPHONE
WIRELESS ROUTER
MP3 PLAYER
JOYSTICK / GAME

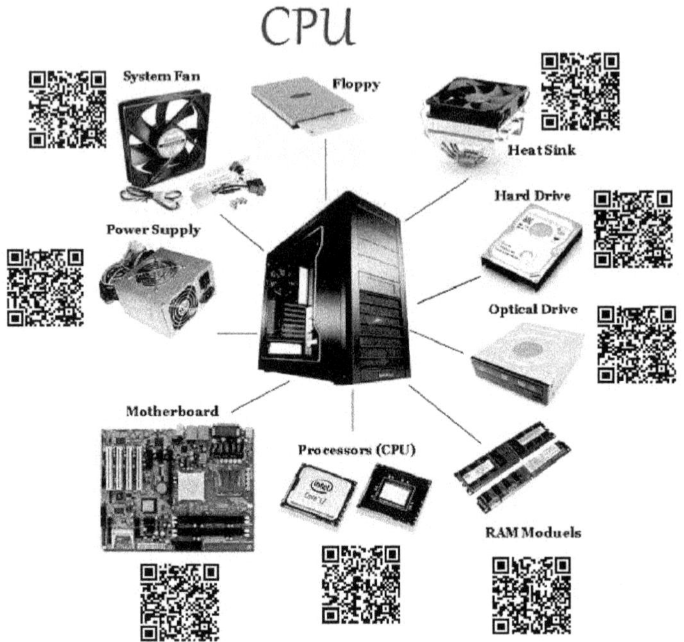


# Computer CPU Hardware Components

# Motherboard Hardware Components

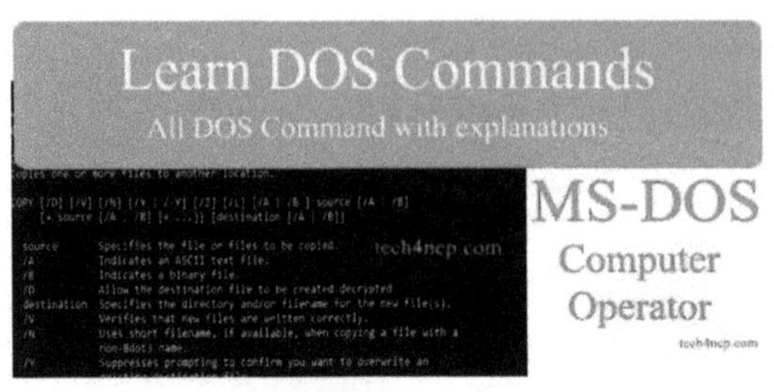

## Excel Basic Functions

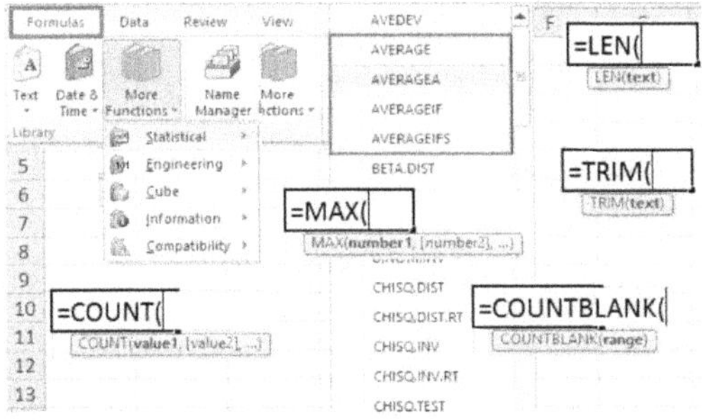

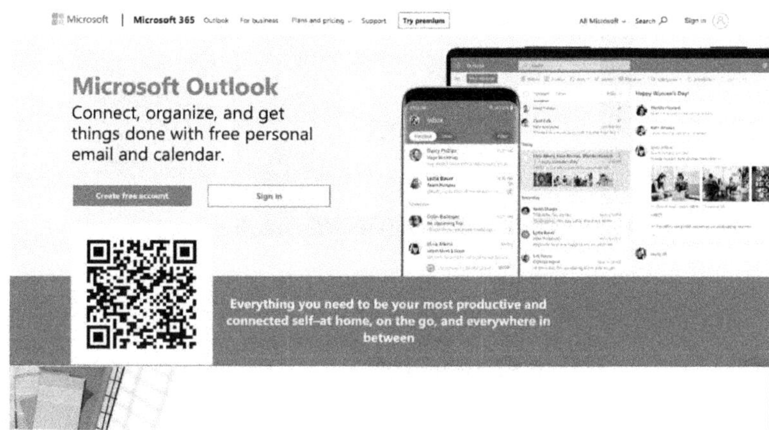
Microsoft
Microsoft 365
Try premium
Microsoft Outlook
Connect, organize, and get things done with free personal email and calendar.
Create free account
Sign in
Everything you need to be your most productive and connected self–at home, on the go, and everywhere in between

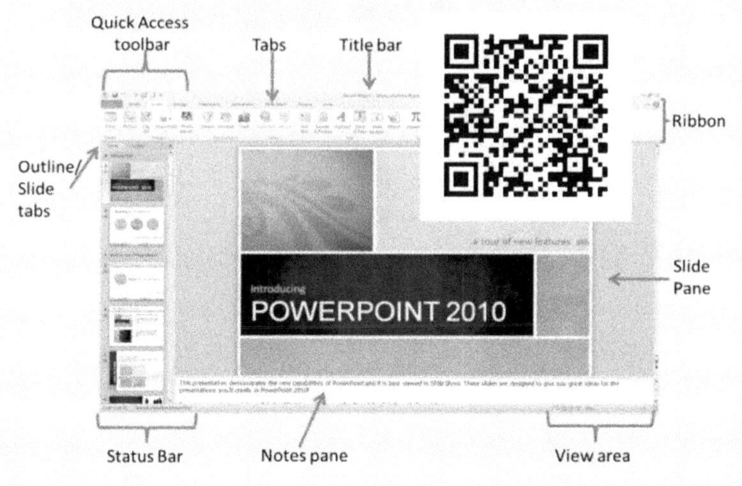
Quick Access toolbar
Tabs
Title bar
Ribbon
Outline/ Slide tabs
Introducing
POWERPOINT 2010
Slide Pane
Status Bar
Notes pane
View area

MS Paint

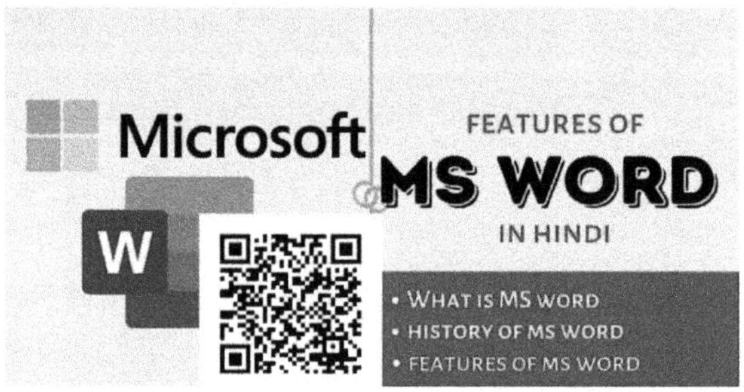
Microsoft
FEATURES OF
MS WORD
IN HINDI
• WHAT IS MS WORD
• HISTORY OF MS WORD
• FEATURES OF MS WORD

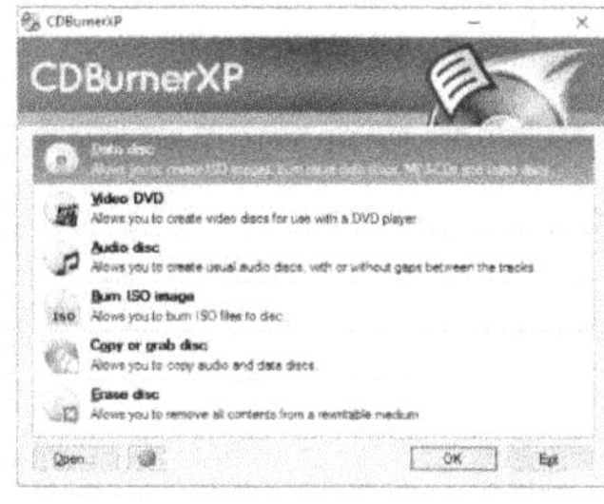
CDBurnerXP
Video DVD
Allows you to create video discs for use with a DVD player
Audio disc
Allows you to create usual audio discs, with or without gaps between the tracks
Burn ISO image
Allows you to burn ISO files to disc.
Copy or grab disc
Allows you to copy audio and data discs.
Erase disc
Allows you to remove all contents from a rewritable medium
OK
Exit

DRIVER
ALLXPSOFT.COM

Top Linux OS
debian
ZORIN OS
KALI

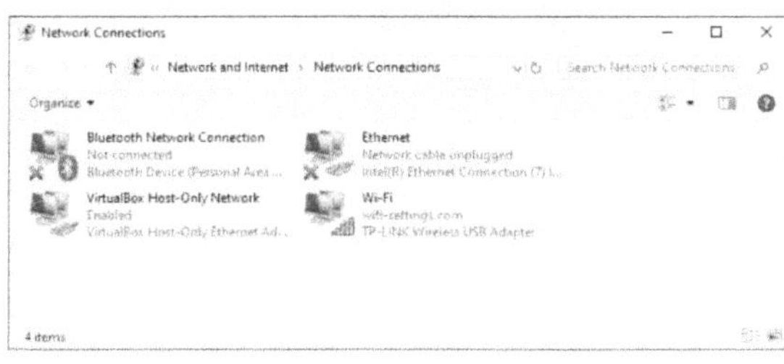
Network Connections
Network and Internet › Network Connections
Organize ▾
Bluetooth Network Connection
Not connected
Ethernet
Network cable unplugged
VirtualBox Host-Only Network
Enabled
Wi-Fi
TP-LINK Wireless USB Adapter
4 items

## Software Installation

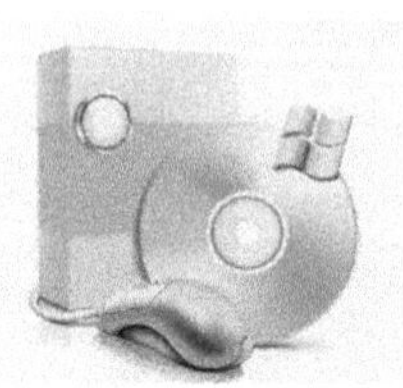

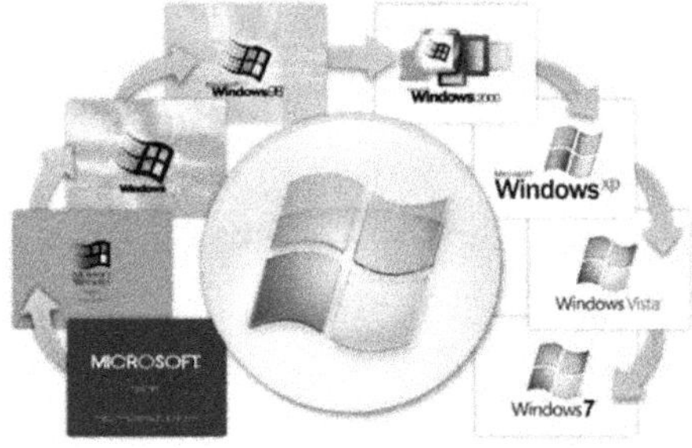

What is
Email?

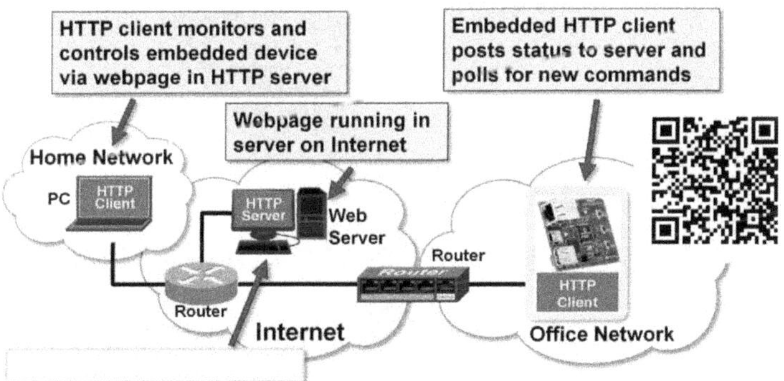
HTTP client monitors and
controls embedded device
via webpage in HTTP server
Embedded HTTP client
posts status to server and
polls for new commands
Webpage running in
server on Internet
Home Network
PC
HTTP
Client
HTTP
Server
Web
Server
Router
Router
Internet
HTTP
Client
Office Network

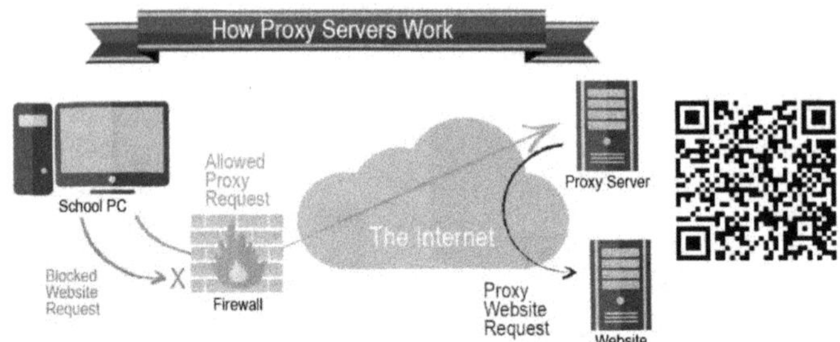
How Proxy Servers Work
School PC
Allowed
Proxy
Request
Blocked
Website
Request
Firewall
The Internet
Proxy Server
Proxy
Website
Request
Website

WWW
What is WWW?

Full HTML & CSS Website
World's Biggest University

CHAPTER NINE

# Mechanical Engineering Carpenter Theory

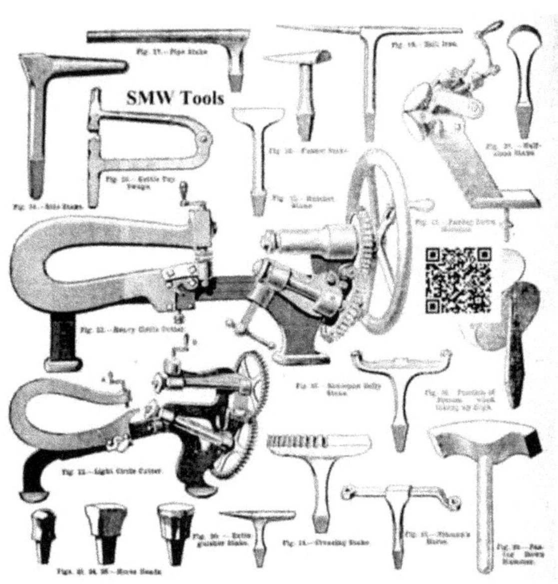
SMW Tools

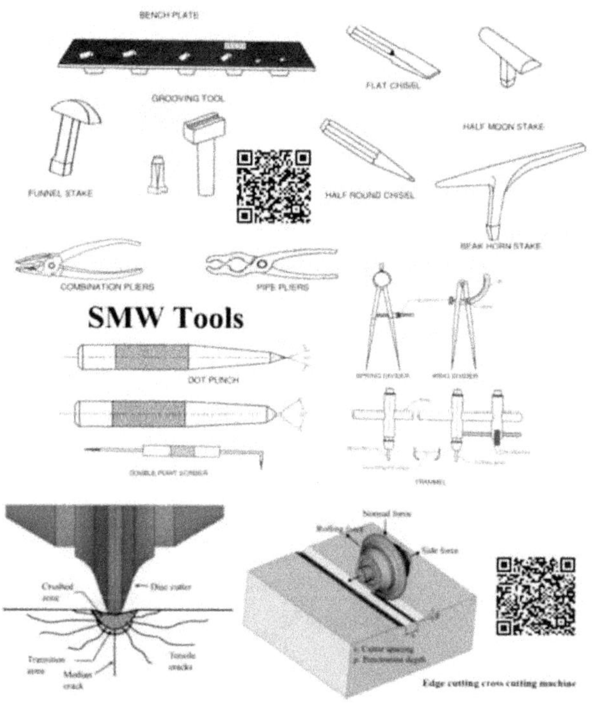
BENCH PLATE
FLAT CHISEL
GROOVING TOOL
HALF MOON STAKE
FUNNEL STAKE
HALF ROUND CHISEL
BEAK HORN STAKE
COMBINATION PLIERS
PIPE PLIERS
SMW Tools
DOT PUNCH
Edge cutting cross cutting machine

Workshop Tools
drill
pipe wrench
monkey wrench
clamp
chisel
anvil
wrench / spanner
shears
ruler
adhesive tape
measuring tape
drill bit
sandpaper
paint brush
toolbox
hacksaw
nail
saw
spirit level
awl
extension cord
hammer
screw
circular saw
screwdriver
chain saw
mallet
glue
file
pliers

CHAPTER TEN

# Mechanical Engineering Plumbing Theory

Workshop Tools
drill
pipe wrench
monkey wrench
clamp
chisel
anvil
wrench / spanner
shears
ruler
adhesive tape
measuring tape
drill bit
sandpaper
paint brush
toolbox
hacksaw
nail
saw
spirit level
awl
extension cord
hammer
screw
circular saw
screwdriver
chain saw
mallet
glue
file
pliers

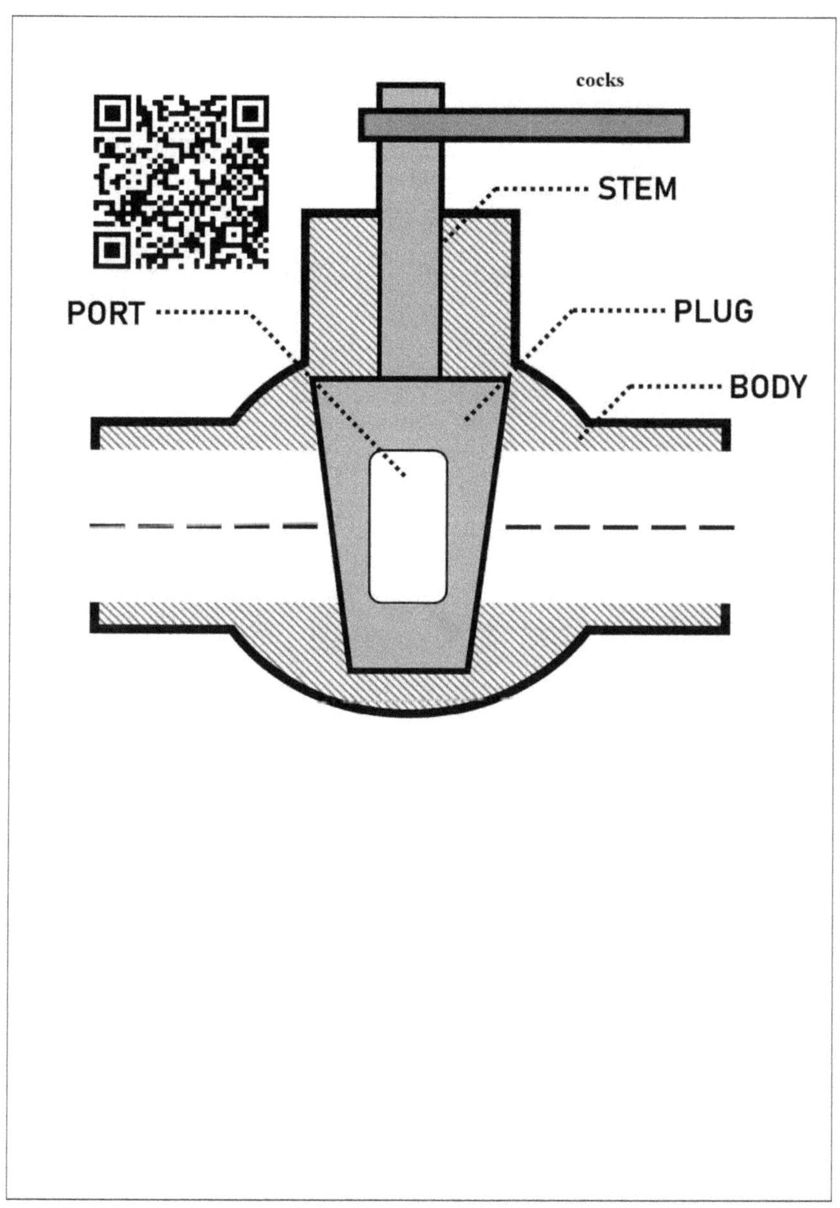
cocks
STEM
PORT
PLUG
BODY

cross
male female elbow
45 deg elbow
hexagon plug
hexagon bushing
hexagon nipples
pipe joints
reducer
welding fitting
socket
hose nipple
lock nut
Flat bottom bend
Pipe joint
Flat bottom bend
Pipe wrench
Forged Hook Jaw
Adjustment Nut
Self-Cleaning Threads
Replaceable, Twice Hardened Alloy Steel Jaws
I-Beam Handle
Hanging Hole

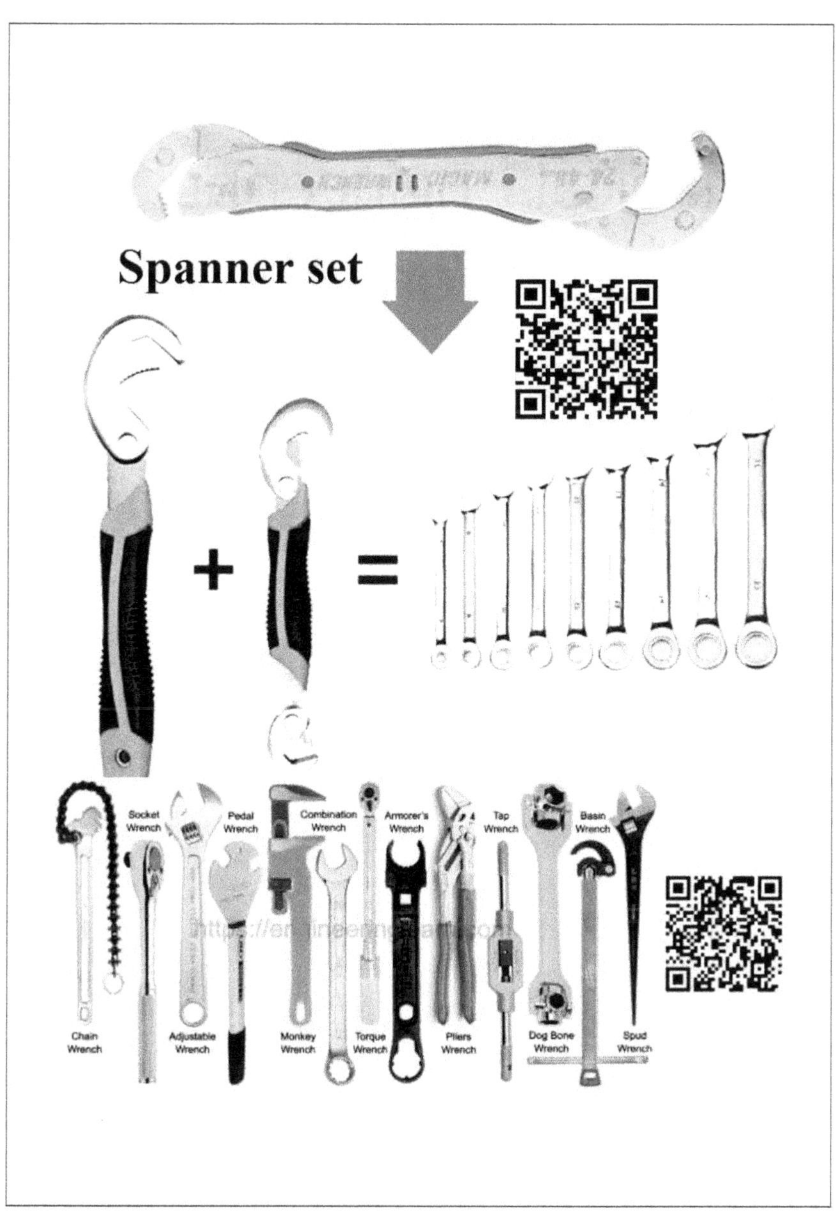


Enter Caption

CHAPTER ELEVEN

# Mechanical Engineering Sheet Metal Work Theory

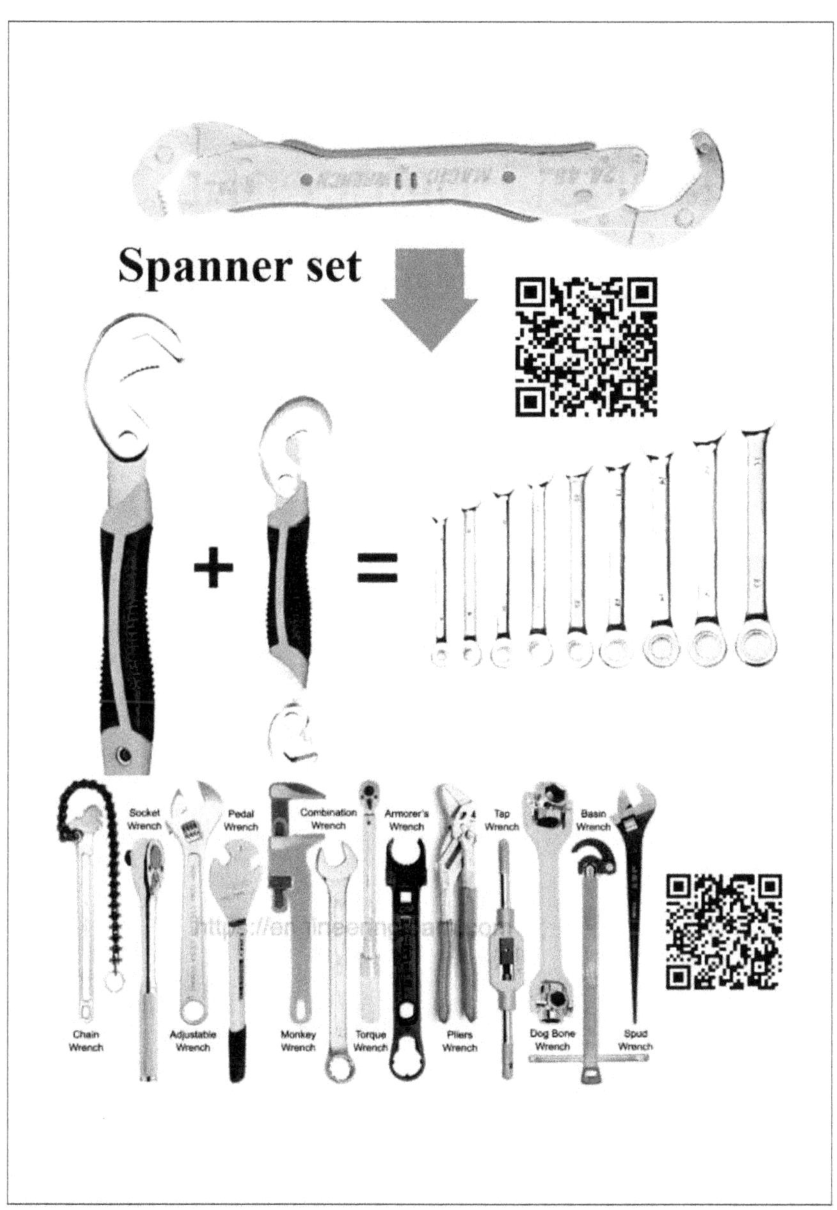


Enter Caption

CHAPTER ELEVEN

# Mechanical Engineering Sheet Metal Work Theory

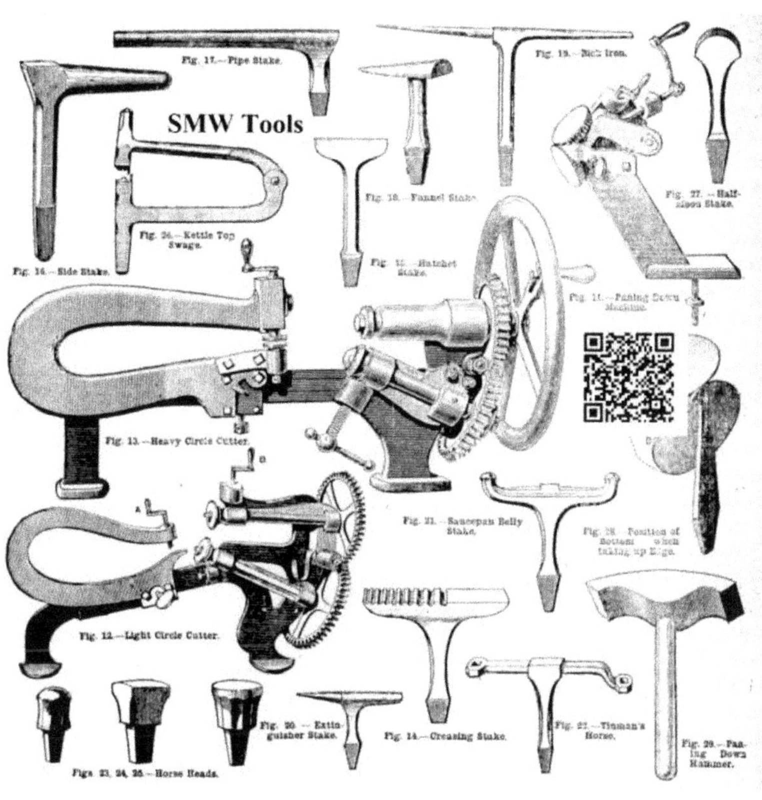
SMW Tools
Fig. 17.—Pipe Stake.
Fig. 16.—Side Stake.
Fig. 26.—Kettle Top Swage.
Fig. 18.—Funnel Stake.
Fig. 15.—Hatchet Stake.
Fig. 27.—Half-moon Stake.
Fig. 11.—Paning Down Machine.
Fig. 13.—Heavy Circle Cutter.
Fig. 21.—Saucepan Belly Stake.
Fig. 12.—Light Circle Cutter.
Figs. 23, 24, 25.—Horse Heads.
Fig. 20.—Extinguisher Stake.
Fig. 14.—Creasing Stake.
Fig. 22.—Tinman's Horse.
Fig. 29.—Paning Down Hammer.

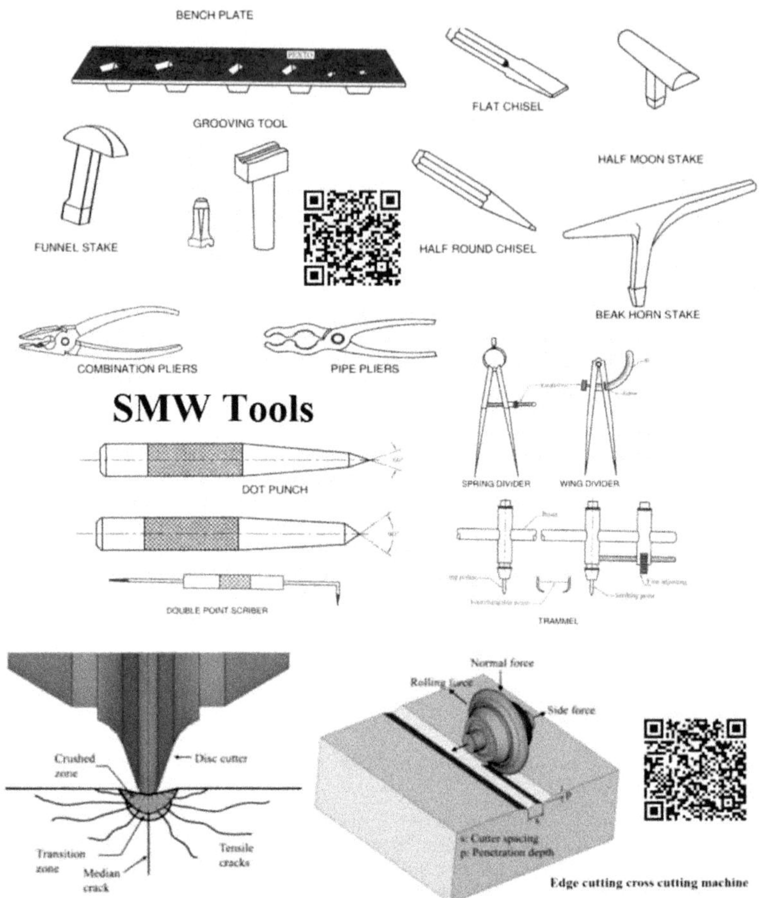
BENCH PLATE
FLAT CHISEL
GROOVING TOOL
HALF MOON STAKE
FUNNEL STAKE
HALF ROUND CHISEL
BEAK HORN STAKE
COMBINATION PLIERS
PIPE PLIERS
SMW Tools
DOT PUNCH
SPRING DIVIDER
WING DIVIDER
DOUBLE POINT SCRIBER
TRAMMEL
Normal force
Rolling force
Side force
Crushed zone
Disc cutter
Transition zone
Median crack
Tensile cracks
s: Cutter spacing
p: Penetration depth
Edge cutting cross cutting machine

CNC Press
Brake Machine

Plate Rolling Machine

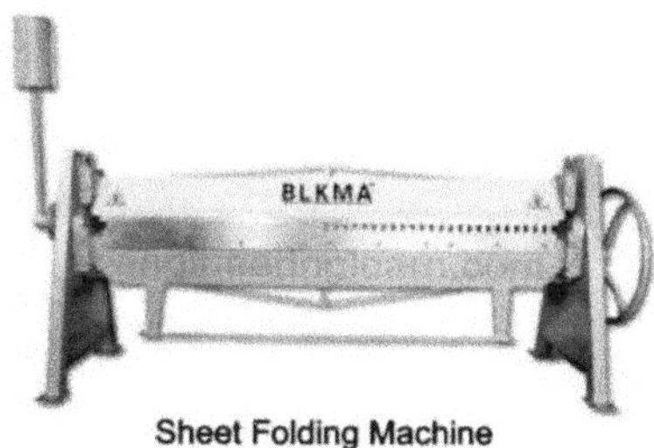

Sheet Folding Machine

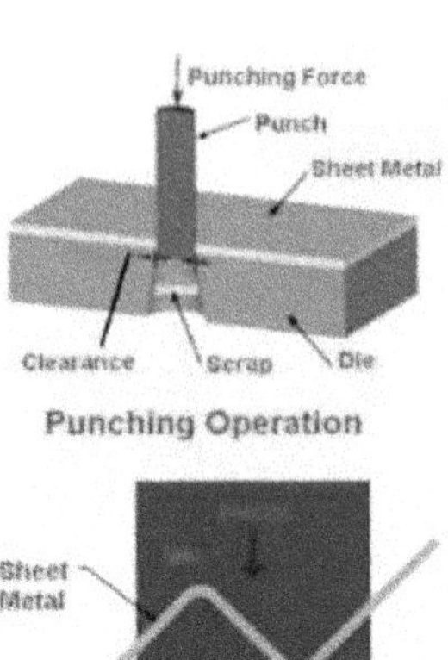

Punching Operation

Offset Bending

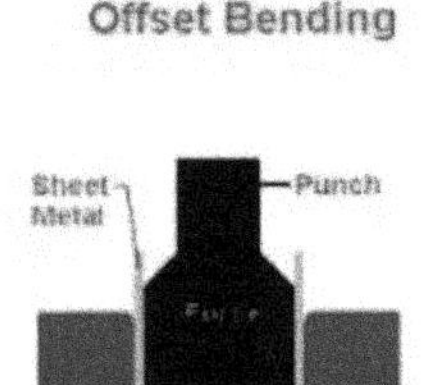

Channel Bending

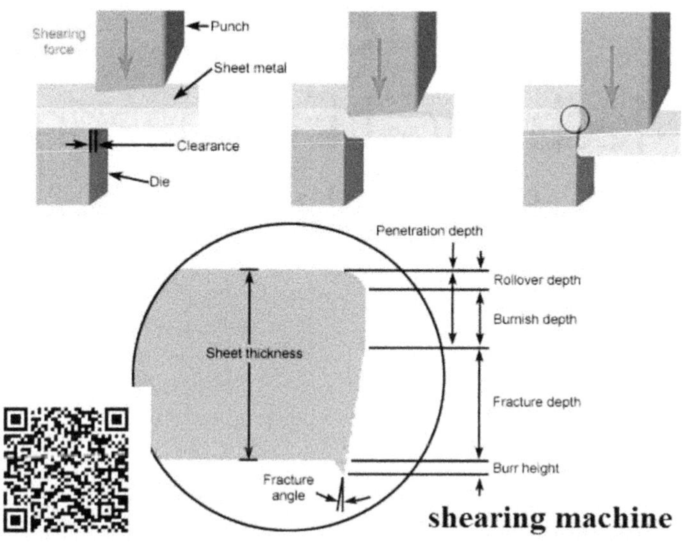


Enter Caption

CHAPTER TWELVE

# Mechanical Engineering Automobile Theory

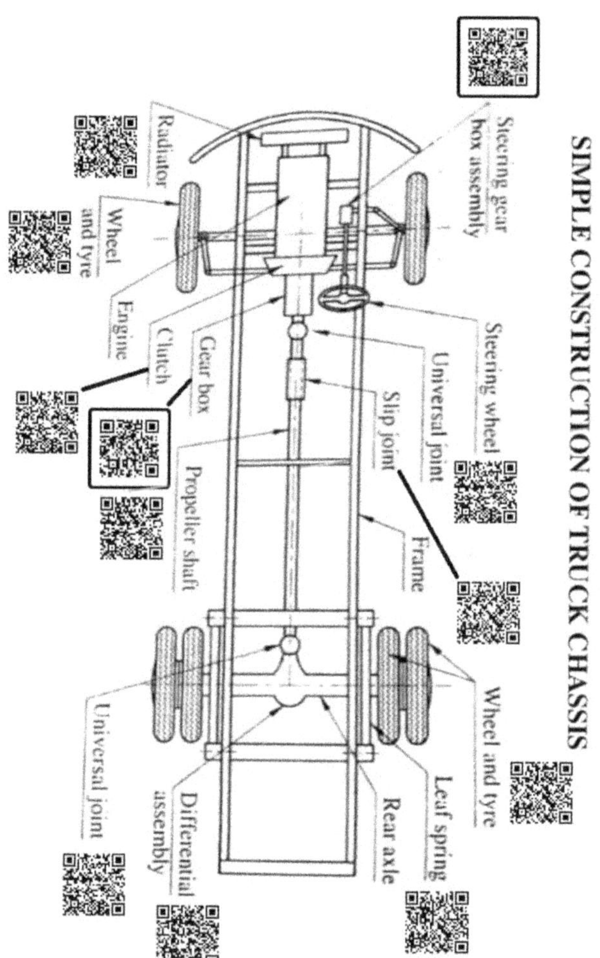
SIMPLE CONSTRUCTION OF TRUCK CHASSIS
Steering gear box assembly
Steering wheel
Universal joint
Slip joint
Frame
Wheel and tyre
Leaf spring
Rear axle
Differential assembly
Universal joint
Propeller shaft
Gear box
Clutch
Engine
Wheel and tyre
Radiator

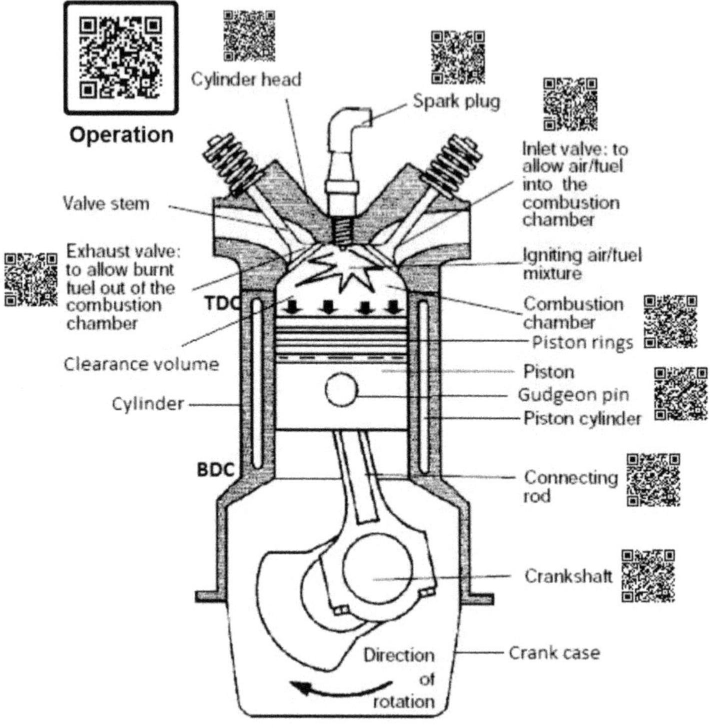


**Petrol Engine Details**

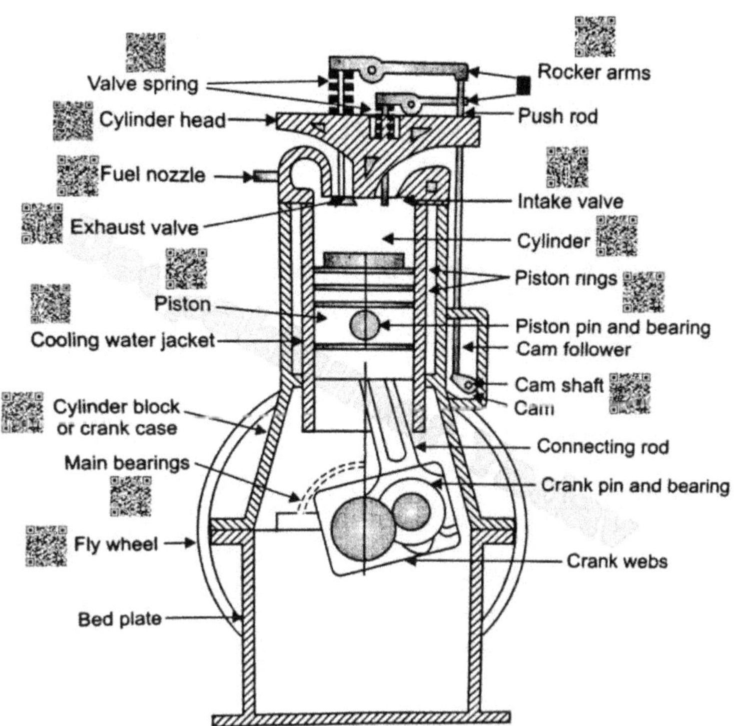


**Components of Diesel Engine**

CHAPTER THIRTEEN

# Mechanical Engineering MCQ

**Safety Precaution in Mechanical Engineering**

01] In case of bleeding, take treatment Of

A] spray cold water

B] Bandage immediately -----]

C] Enquire about the accident thought treatment

D] cold 3" and rest

02] in case of an accident, the victim should im

A] Asked to take rest

C] Attended immediately

D] leave him

03] First aid is given to an injured or ill person primarily....

A] Save life

B] Prevent further deterioration of the muff's

C] Give best possible comfort

D] All of these

04] Colour code for Bins for waste paper segregation is -----

A] blue Colour

B] Yellow Colour

C] Red Colour

D] Green Colour

05] In Japanese Seiko stands for -------------

A] Shine

B] Sort

C] Standardize

D] Sustain

06] Benefit of SS system is ------

A] Increase in productivity

B] Increase in quality

C] Reduction in wastage of time

D] All of these

07] Safety is -----------

A] nobody's business

B] every bodise business

C] Some bodies business

D] The organization business

08] For basic categories of safety signs are available The meaning of"prohibition" sign ----

A] shows it must not be done

B] Shows what must be done

C] Warns the hazard or danger

D] Gives information of safety provision

09] Which one is a workshop safety?

A] Keep shop floor clean and free from grease, oil or other slippery materials

B] Stop the machine before changing the speed

C] Don't use cracked or chipped tools

D] Don't try to stop a running machine with hand

10] In Personal Protect Equipment (PPE] HELMET is used to

A] protect head

B] Protect eyes

C] Protect hands

D] Protect ears

11] Which of the following belongs to general safety?

A Have a worker in good attitude

B] The work clean and clear

C] Concentrate on your work

D] Keep the floor and gangways clean and clear

12] While grinding, which is used to protect the eyes?

A] Dark green glass

B] Mask

C] Sun glasses

D] Safety goggles

13] Which of the following is done for machine safety?

A] Check the oil level before starting the machine

B] Do things in a methodical way

C] Keep the floor and gangways clean and clear

D] Don't use dies and scarves

14] In Personal Protect Equipment (PPE], 'sleeves' is used to protect ----------

A] Face

B] Eyes

C] Ears

D] Hands

15] ABC stands for --------------

A] Automatic Breathing Control

B] Automatic Blood Control

C] Airway Breathing Circulation

D] Automatic Blood Circulation

16] To put off"Class B" fire, the types of fire extinguisher used is ...........]

A] dry power

B] Carbon dioxide

C] Jet of water

D] Foam type

17] Which type of fire extinguisher is used to put off general fire?

A] Water type Extinguisher

B] Foam type Extinguisher

C] Dry chemical powder Extinguisher

D] Carbon dioxide (C02] Extinguisher

**Hand Tools in Mechanical Engineering**

18] One micrometer (U] is equal to...

A] 0.1mm

B] 0.01mm

C] 0.001mm

D] 0.0001mm

19] Name the tool used to make and finish the leak proof joints of a pipe T joint

A] groover

B] setting hammer

C] creasing hammer

D] round bottom stake

20] Portion of the hammer used for fixing the handle is...

A] Face

B] Peen

C] Cheek

D] Eye hole

21] Weight of the hammer for the marking purpose is...

A] 250g

B] 500g

C] 1 kg

D] 2 kgs

22] To cut out small apertures which punch and die type of machine is used?

A] shear type nibbler

B] punch type nibbler

C] circular cutting machine

D] guillotine shearing machine

23] Scribers are made of...

A] Mild steel

B] High carbon steel

C] Brass

D] Cast iron

24] The size of an engineer's vice is specified by the...

A] Length of the movable jaw

B] Width of the jaws

C] Height of the vice

D] Maximum opening of the jaws

vice Bench vice

Bench Vice

25] The form of thread used in carpenters vice is...

A] Square

B] Acme thread

C] Sawtooth Thread

D] Knuckle thread

26] The convexity of files helps...

A] To file concave surfaces

B] To file convex surfaces

C] To prevent rounding of edges of work

D] The file to become straight when pressure is applied

27]] Name the instrument used to check the perpendicularity of the branch pipe with the main pipe of a pipe T joint

A] protractor

B] try square

C] spirit level

D] straight edge

28] The caliper meant for measuring the width of a slot is...

A] Odd leg caliper

B] Outside caliper

C] Jenny caliper

D] Inside calliper

29] The included angle of the groove of 'V' block is always....

A] $45^{\circ}$

B] $60^{\circ}$

C] $90^{\circ}$

D] $120^{\circ}$

v blocks

v block

'V' blocks

30] 'V' blocks are available in grades of...

A] A & B

B] A,B & C

C] 1,2 & 3

D] 1 & 2

31] 'V' blocks of grade 'B' are made of

A] Cast iron

B] Mild steel

C] Steel

D] Cast steel

32] 'V' block 50/5-40 A is used for holding jobs of diameter

A] Ø 50 mm

B] Ø 5 to Ø 50 mm

C] Ø 5 to Ø 40 mm

D] Ø 40 mm

33] The reason for using cast iron in making 'V' blocks

A] to increase the weight of the block

B] to reduce the cost

C] to reduce the friction

D] to get a good appearance

34] For cutting thin tubing, the most suitable pitch of the hacksaw blade is...

A] 1.8mm

B] 1.4mm

C] 1mm

D] 0.8mm

35] For cutting solid brass, the most suitable pitch of the hacksaw blade is...

A] 1.8mm

B] 1.4mm

C] 1mm

D] 0.8mm

36] A new hacksaw blade after a few strokes becomes loose because of the...

A] Stretching of the blade

B] Wing-nut threads being worn out

C] Wrong pitch of the blade

D] Improper selection of the set of saws.

37] While cutting small diameter pipes, it is advisable to watch regularly and ensure that...

A] The cut is along the curved line

B] More saw teeth are in contract

C] The work is not overheated

D] Proper balancing of hacksaw is maintained

**Drilling in Mechanical Engineering**

38] If the drill runs untrue, it will

A] get too hot

B] cut undersize

C] distort the spindle

D] cut an oversized hole

39] Running the drill too fast many result in

A] spoiling the cutting edge

B] poor surface finish

C] twisting the tang

D] drilling an oval hole

40] A drill with worn land will

A] drill hole oversize

B] drill hole undersize

C] run out of centre

D] drill an accurate hole

41] The morse taper provided on drills used on lathe ranges between

A] MT1 to MT5

B] MT1 to MT4

C] MT0 to MT5

D] MT0 to MT4

42] Feeding the small drill too fast into the work may result in

A] breaking the drill

B] bending the drill

C] cutting an oval shape hole

D] increased production

43] The drill size for a M 20 tap is

A] 17.5 mm

B] 18 mm

C] 18.5 mm

D] 19 mm

44] The taper shank drills are held on the machine by means of...

A] Chucks

B] Sleeves

C] Drift

D] Vice

45] Drill chucks are fitted on the drilling machine spindle by means of a...

A] Knurled ring

B] Arbor

C] Drift

D] Pinion and key

drill chuck

drilling

Drill Chuck

46] The Morse taper provided on drills ranges between...

A] MT 1 to MT 5

B] MT 1 to MT 4

C] MT 0 to MT 5

D] MT 0 to MT 4

47] A drift is used for...

A] Drawing a drill location

B] Fixing chuck on the machine spindle

C] Removing a broken drill from the work

D] Removing the drill from the machine spindle

48] When the taper shank of the drill is larger than the machine spindle, the device to hold the drill is a...

A] Drill sleeve

B] Taper socket

C] Drill drift

D] Chuck and key

49] A special feature of the radial drilling machine is...

A] It can be used for drilling with a H.S.S] drill
B] Table can be moved and set at any position
C] A variety of speeds is available
D] The spindle can be brought to any position
50] The point angle of drills depends on...
A] The size of the drill
B] The type of machine
C] The material of the work
D] The RPM of the drill
51] The point angle for a standard drill is...
A] 60◦
B] 108◦
C] 118◦
D] 135◦
52] The helical angle determines the...
A] Cutting angle
B] Chew angle
C] Rake angle
D] Lip angle
53] The clearance angle of the drill is between...
A] 3◦ to 5◦
B] 8◦ to 12◦
C] 12◦ to 20◦
D] 15◦ to 20◦
54] The relief angle provided behind the cutting edge is called the..
A] Point angle
B] Chisel edge angle
C] Helix angle
D] Clearance angle
55] A set of number drill series consists of drills in the following ranges] Indicate the correct range
A] 1 to 40
B] 1 to 50
C] 1 to 80
D] 1 to 100
56] In the number drill series, the smallest drill size is...
A] 0.1 mm

B] 0.35 mm

C] 0.5 mm

D] 0.52 mm

57] In the number drill series, the largest drill size is...

A] 102 mm

B] 5.791 mm

C] 5.613 mm

D] 5.410 mm

58] In the letter drill series, the size of the drill 'A' is equal to ...

A] 13 mm

B] 6.08 mm

C] 6.045 mm

D] 5.944 mm

59] In the letter drill series, the largest drill size is equal to...

A] 10.33 mm

B] 10.490 mm

C] 12.01 mm

D] 15.00 mm

60] In a remote place ( no electricity available] a rail track is to be drilled] Choose the right drilling machine

A] Radial drilling machine

B] Pillar drilling machine

C] Ratchet drilling machine

D] Sensitive drilling Machine

61] A drilling machine used by a carpenter for cabinet making is a...

A] Ratchet drilling machine

B] Radial drilling machine

C] Breast drilling machine

D] Sensitive drilling machine

62] Surface plates are made of...

A] High grade cast steel

B] Fine-grained cast iron

C] Alloy steels

D] Wrought iron

63] The drill size for a M 20 tap is

A] 17.5 mm

B] 18 mm

C] 18.5 mm

D] 19 mm

64] Tapping is mostly done to produce

A] external 'V' thread

B] <u>internal 'V' thread</u>

C] external square thread

D] internal square thread

65] The drill size for tapping is

A] more than the tap size

B] <u>less than the tap size</u>

C] equal to the tap size

D] either more or less than the tap size

66] which one of the following is the most suitable tap for lathe work?

A] spiral tap

B] <u>machine tap</u>

C] hand tap

D] left hand tap

67] A die is turned with a

A] die wrench

B] <u>diestock</u>

C] die plate

D] die handle

68] A tumbler gear unit has

A] a single gear

B] two gears

C] <u>three gears</u>

D] four gears

69] The cutting edge of a solid tool is made of

A] <u>carbon steel</u>

B] mild steel

C] super high speed steel

D] stelite

70] The tip of a cemented carbide threading tool is

A] <u>brazed</u>

B] welded

C] soldered

D] clamped to the shank

71] Tool will rub against the work surfaces and the cutting force increases when..

A] The clearance angle is more

B] The clearance angel is less

C] The rake angle is more

D] The rake angle is less

72] Formation of a chip while cutting is based on the...

A] Rake angle of the tool

B] Clearance angle of the tool

C] Wedge angle of the tool

D] Clearance and wedge angle of the tool

73] The suitable cutting fluid for drilling mild steel in a drilling machine is...

A] Synthetic soluble oil

B] Neat oil

C] Distilled water

D] Soluble oil

74] Centre drilling is an operation of...

A] Drilling and countersinking

B] Drilling and counter boring

C] Marking the centre location before drilling

D] Enlarging the diameter of a hole

75] Shaft ends are centre drilled for...

A] Supporting jobs between centres

B] Lubricating the dead centre

C] Reducing the weight

D] Assisting counter boring

76] The Centre drill size is selected on the basis of the

A] length of the job

B] material of the job

C] diameter of the job

D] type of operation

77] Centre drilling is done at a

A] high spindle speed with a high feed

B] low spindle speed with a high feed

C] high spindle speed with a low feed

D] low spindle speed with a low feed

**Measuring Instruments in Mechanical Engineering**

78] The least count of vernier caliper is

A] 0.01 mm

B] <u>0.02mm</u>

C] 0.001 mm

D] 0.2 mm

vernier caliper

vernier caliper

Vernier Caliper

79] The graduations of a depth micrometer are...

A] Similar to an outside micrometer

B] <u>In the reverse direction to that of the outside micrometer, both Thimble and sleeve</u>

C] In the reverse direction only on the sleeve

D] In the direction only on the thimble

depth micrometer

depth micrometer

Depth Micrometer

80] The process of enlarging the end of a hole for accommodating the socket screw head is...

A] Reaming

B] Spot facing

C] Counter boring

D] Counter sinking

boring

Boring Operation

81]While choosing a boring tool for boring a given diameter, select

A] a long tool

B] a short tool

C] a long and stout tool

D] a short and stout tool

82] The cutting edge of the boring tool should be set for a small hole so that it is

A] 0.5 mm above the center

B] 0.5 mm below the center

C] 1 mm above the center

D] in the exact center

83] Bored holes are to be chamfered by using

A] a drill

B] triangular scraper

C] a cranked boring tool

D] a flat file

84] The tool used for boring deep holes is a

A] lathe mandrel

B] sleeve

C] drill

D] boring bar

E] auger bit

85] The cutting speed for rough boring is the

A] same as rough turning

B] same as drilling

C] same as knurling

D] same as thread cutting

86] The reamer is used for...

A] Drilling holes in thin sheets

B] Drilling deep holes

C] Removing burrs

D] Enlarging and finishing holes

reamer

reamer

Reamer

87] The reamer teeth are unevenly spaced because...

A] They are easy to manufacture

B] They can reduce chattering

C] They help to cut metal gradually

D] They help to remove the reamer easily

88] Which among the following is not a capability of reamers?

A] Finishing small holes

B] Finishing any machined profiles

C] Accuracy to closer limits

D] Producing high quality surface finish

89] The most important quality of any cutting fluid is

A] emulsification

B] specific heat

C] specific gravity

D] viscosity

# cutting fluid 1

## Cutting Fluid

90] By using coolants on workpieces we can choose

A] higher cutting speeds

B] lowcr cutting feeds

C] lower cutting speeds

D] heavy depth of cuts

91] The cutting speed for aluminium with H.S.S] tools is

A] 30 m/min

B] 50 m/min

C] 70 m/min

D] 130 m/min

92] The cutting speed for brass with a H.S.S] tool is

A] 10 m/min

B] 25 m/min

C] 70 m/min

D] 140 m/min

93] The distance, which the cutting edge of a tool passes over the material in a minute while machining is Know as...

A] RPM

B] Feed

C] Machine speed

D] Cutting speed

94] The cutting angle for chipping cast iron is...

A] $37.5^{\circ}$

B] $55^{\circ}$

C] $60^{\circ}$

D] $90^{\circ}$

95] The depth of cut is given by

A] the top slide
B] the cross-slide
C] the compound slide
D] adjusting the tool
96] For mounting a lathe chuck
A] start it by hand and then turn the power on
B] mount it on by power
C] mount it by hand
D] mount it with the help of a hammer

lathe chucks

lathe chuck

Lathe Four Jaw Chuck

97] The morse taper provided on drills used on lathe ranges between
A] MT1 to MT5
B] MT1 to MT4
C] MT0 to MT5
D] MT0 to MT4
98] Feeding the small drill too fast into the work may result in
A] breaking the drill
B] bending the drill

C] cutting an oval shape hole

D] increased production

99] Number of flutes in a twist drills are --------

A] 1

B] 2

C] 3

D] 4

100] Which one of the following drilling machines is used for drilling holes where electricity is not available?

A] Bench drilling machine

B] Pillar drilling machine

C] Redial drilling machine

D] Ratchet drilling machine

101] Which one of the following drilling machine is used for heavy duty work?

A] Bench drilling machine

B] Pillar drilling machine

C] Radial drilling machine

D] Electric hand drilling machine

102] The suitable cutting fluid for drilling mild steel in a lathe is

A] synthetic soluble oil

B] neat cutting oil

C] distilled water

D] soluble oil+water

103] The suitable cutting fluid for precision grinding is

A] Soluble oil

B] Synthetic soluble oil

C] Neat oil

D] Servo Cut's'

gringing wheel grinding wheel

Grinding Wheel

104] Advantage of using cutting fluid during grinding operation is ------

A] 5000 surface finish

B] Reduction in cutting forces

C] Reduction in hardening of the work piece

D] All of these]

105] Lubricant is necessary to ............]

A] run the machine smoothly taking least load

B] Run the machine quickly

C] Stop the machine immediately

D] Produce work piece of greater accuracy

106] The main purpose for using a lubricant in machine tools is to ------

A] Cool down the making parts

B] Prevent machine tool from heating

C] Wet the making parts for close contact

D] Minimize the friction between the making parts

107] Driving plates are used for

A] mounting fixtures and workpieces

B] driving shafts between Centre's with a lathe dog

C] facing operations only

D] internal operations only

108] Balancing is done in the face plate work

A] to increase the speed

B] to reduce the pressure on the tool

C] for uniform rotation of work

D] to get a good finish

109] A face plate is used to hold

A] a round job

B] a finished job

C] an irregular Job

D] a hollow job

110] Which is correct angle plate used with face plate

(A] Solid Type

(B] Box Type

(C] Adjustable Type

(D] None of them

angle plate

Angle Plate

111] Face plate is made from.....]

(A] Mild Steel

(B] Cast Iron

(C] Brass

(D] Aluminium

112] Which following accessories is use for odd an uneven job turning?

(A] Three Jaw Chuck

(B] Two Jaw Chuck

(C] Driving Plate

(D] Face Plate

113] An irregular shaped work piece is turned on a Lathe] Which one of the following work holding accessories is used?

A] Two Jaw chuck

B] Three Jaw chuck

C] Driving plate

D] Face plate

114]The pads of a steady rest are made of

A] carbon steel

B] lead

C] mild steel

D] brass

steady rest

Steady Rest

115] A steady rest is used

A] to hold jobs

B] for face plate work

C] to drive the job

D] <u>to support the job</u>

116] A follower steady is held on the

A] lathe bed

B] <u>lathe carriage</u>

C] lathe spindle

D] tailstock

117] When turning long work pieces, the following is used

A sleeve

B change gear

<u>C steady rest</u>

D bracket]

118] Knurling operation is done at the

A] turning spindle speed

B] high spindle speed

C] <u>1/3 of the turning spindle speed</u>

D] 1/2 of the turning spindle speed

knurling tool

Knurling Tool

119] Knurling is the operation of

A] shearing

B] forming

C] turning

D] pressing

120] Mandrels are generally used when machining with

A] heavy cuts

B] short facing cuts

C] light cuts

D] boring tools

**Limit Fit & Tolerances in Mechanical Engineering**

121] In the B.I.S system 25 hole deviations are specified by

A] small letters

B] small letters with numbers

C] small letters with tolerance

D] capital letters

122] The standard range of sizes covered in the B.I.S] system of limits and fits are

A] 0 to 10 mm

B] 0 to 100 mm

C] 25 to 400 mm

D] 0 to 500 mm

123] The basic size is the size

A] mentioned in the drawing

B] machined by the operator

C] based on which deviations are given

D] given by the instructor

124] Limits of size are

A] 2

B] 3

C] 4

D] 5

125] The number of fundamental deviations in the B.I.S] system are

A] 20

B] 22

C] 25

D] 28

126] The number of grade of tolerances in the B.I.S] system are

A] 12

B] 16

C] 18

D] 20

127] The size based on which the dimensional deviations are given is called...

A] Actual size

B] Basic size

C] Minimum limit of size

D] Maximum limit of Size

128] The size of parts made by .....] for provide interchange ability properties] (A] Measurement System

(B] Trial and Error System

(C] Limit and Tolerance System

(D] None of Them

129] Your job taper is correct if it is measured

A above the higher limit

B in between higher and lower limit

C below the lower limit]

130] When tolerance given in one side of the basic dimension, it is called --------

A].Tolerance system

B] Unilateral tolerance

C] Bilateral tolerance

D] Allowance System

131] A dimension is stated as (025 H7 in a drawing] The lower limit is -----------

A] 24.75 mm

B] 24.85 mm

C] 25.00 mm

D] 25-021 mm

132] The measured Size Of the dimensions of a component as called---------

A] Basic size

B] Nominal Size

C] Allowed size

D] Actual size

133] In the drawing the dimensions of a shaft is shown 40i 0068/0042, which is the size of Shaft within the tolerance?

A] 4.0.64 mm

B] 40.042 mm

C] 40.000 mm

D] 39.998 mm

134] In Hole basic system ----------

A] The size of the shaft is made constant

B] The Size of the hole is made constant

C] Only 'allowance is given on the hole

D] The permissible tolerance are given on the hole and the Shaft

135] The Size of a component is given as 24 -0.1] What does -O.1 indicates? _

A] Upper deviation is + 0.1 mm ]

B] Lower deviation is 0.0 mm

C] Fundamental deviation is 0.0 mm

D] Lower deviation is _0.1 mm

136] The tolerance of a hole iS the difference between the -------

A] Maximum hole Size and maximum Shaft size

B] Maximum hole size and maximum hole Size

C] Minimum'hole size and maximum Shaft Size

D] Minimum hole Size and minimum shaft Size

137] A hole whose lower deviation is zero is called basic hole] Which one of the following letter indicates basic hole? ]

A] E

B] F

C] G '

D] H

138] Which one having upper deviation zero?

A] Bassc Shaft

B] Basic hole

C] Tolerance

D] Clearance

139] A ball bearing on a shaft is type of fit? ,

A] Clearance fit

B] Driving fit

C] Shrinkage fit

D] None of the above

140] Which one of the following is important factor required to achieve the interchange ability in mass production? ]

A] Geometrical accuracy]

B] Standardization

C] Dimensional accuracy

D] Surface finish

141] In the BIS system of limits and fits, the grade of tolerance are represented by number Symbols and there are ---------i

A] 14 grades of tolerance

B] 16 grades of tolerance

C] 18 grades of tolerance ‘

D] 20 grades of tolerance

142] A Product is said to have the quality when ...........]

A] Its shape and dimensions are within the limit

B] It is fit for use

C] It appears to be very good

D] The choice of material is right

143] The maximum clearance required between hole’30 +0.021, 0.000 and shaft 30 -0.110, 0.143 is.

A] 0.110 mm ‘

B]0.131 mm

C] 0.164 mm

D] 0.143 mm

144] A dimension is stated as 25 .1002 mm in a drawing] What is the tolerance?

A] +0.02 mm’

B] +0.04 mm

C] -0.02 mm

D] 25.00 mm

145] A pin is fitted in a hole] The tolerance zone of the pin is entirely above that of hole] The fit obtained will be?

A] Clearance fit

B] Transition fit

C] Interference fit

D] Running fit

146] Interchange ability is normally applied for? _

A] Repairing of parts

B] Mass production

C] Single piece production

D] All of these

147] Tolerance is given to the part size to...........]

A] Production the part within the required permissible size error

B] Increase the production

C] Decrease the Production

D] Finish the components approximately

148] Which one of the following is the clearance fit under the whole basic system?

A] 20 H7/p6'

B] 2067/211

C] ZOG/gll ]

D] 20H/g11]

149] The three classes of fits as per BIS system aré ...........] ~ ]

A] Clearance fit, interference fit and transition fit

B] Medium fit, push fit and tight fit

C] Flat fit, round fit and square fit

D] 'Sliding fit ', loose fit and shrinkage fit

150] Which one of the following tolerance specifications has a maximum dimensionless than 20 mm?

A] 20 +0.2,-0.3

B] 20 320.2

C] 20 -0.2, 0.3 e

D]m 20 +500, ~03

151] Difference between the maximum and minimum limit is -~-~~~~-~~~~~ '

A] Single informant

B] Basic shaft

C] Clearance

D] Tolerance

152] A shaft 55 running freely in bush bearing the type of fit is ---------

A] Clearance fit

B] Driving plate

C] shrinkage fit

D] None of the above

153] The taper ratio of the morse taper is

A] 1 in 10

B] 1 in 15

C] 1 in 20

D] 1 in 25

154] The morse standard taper is available in

A] 16 Nos

B] 12 Nos

C] 10 Nos

D] 8 Nos

155] Taper turning by offsetting the tailstock method can produce

A] an internal taper

B] an internal taper thread

C] an external taper

D] both external and internal tapers

taper turning

taper turning attachment

Taper by Tailstock Offset

156] By using the taper turning attachment, tapers can be turned with a setting angle up to

A] 10°

B] 15°

C] 20◦

D] 30◦

157] The accuracy of a taper is generally checked by means of......

A] taper gauges

B] gauge blocks

C] indicator and height gauge

D] 'V' blocks

158] Turning tapers by the compound rest method involves working solely with

Decimal measurements

B fractional measurements

C metric measurements

D angular measurements]

159] Long tapers are produced

A with the taper turning attachment

B with the compound slide

C by setting over the tail stock

D by adjusting the cross slide]

160] The length of turned tapers are checked with

A vernier calliper

B micrometer

C inside callper

D dial test indicator]

161] The disadvantages of taper turning using the com] pound slide are

A] only long tapers can be turned

B] only very large tapers can be turned

C] only manual in feed is possible

D] only short tapers can be turned due to the restrictions of the compound slide]

162] External tapers are checked with

A] limit plug gauge

B] taper ring gauge

C ]taper plug gauge

D] thread plug gauge]

163] The use of a taper turned on lathe is ----

A] Assist to transmit drive in the assembled parts

B] Used for Assembly and disassembly of parts

C] Give self alignment in the assembled parts

164] Which type of method is used in mass production of production of producing small length of taper?

A] Form tool

B] Compound slide

C] Tailstock offset.

D] Taper turning attachment

165] Morse standard taper is one of the internationally accepted standards taper, which is available in numbers from--------

A]1to7

B]1 to 8

C] O to 7

D] 0 to 8

166] Which taper turning method is used for cutting steep taper?

A] Set over method

B] Taper turning attachment

C] Form tool

D] Swivelling the compound rest

167] Morse taper is used in which of the following machine components -...

A] Spindles of lathe

B] Spindles of drill machine

C] Shanks of reamers

D] All of these

168] For mass production of the taper which one of the following method is used.......]

A] Tailstock offset method

B] Taper turning attachment method

C] Form too method

D] Compound slide method

169] The major diameter of the taper is 40 mm, minor diameter is 30 mm] The total length of the job is 100 mm is tapered then offset is given by -

A] 5 mm

B] 7.5 mm

C] 12 mm

D] 9 mm

170] The accuracy of an ordinary bevel protractor is --' ------------degree]

A] One

B] Three

C] Two

D] Four

171] The least count of a vernier bevel protractor is...

A] 1”

B] 5’

C] 1◦

D] 5 ◦

172] The part of a vernier bevel protractor which is normally used as a reference base for measuring angles is the...

A] Blade

B] Stock

C] Disc

C] Main scale

173] The part of a vernier bevel protector on which main scale divisions are marked is the...

A] Stock

B] Dial

C] Disc

D] Adjustable blade

174] The part of a bevel protractor, which comes in contact with the inclined surface while measuring is the...

A] Blade

B] Stock

C] Disc

D] Dial

175] The value of each division of the main scale of a vernier bevel protractor is...

A] 5’

B] 1◦

C] 5◦

D.10◦

176] The value of each division of the vernier scale of a bevel protractor is...

A] 1◦

B] 1◦5’

C] 1◦55’

D.5'

177] The part of the vernier bevel protractor on which main scale divisions are marked

A stock

B dial

C disc

D adjustable blade

178] In Vernier bevel protractor is designed to measure?

A] Acute angles

B] Obtuse angles

C] Acute and Obtuse angle

D] Liner dimensions

179] To get least count of 5 in a vernier bevel protractor the 23° main scale are divided into -..

A] 12 equal parts on vernier scale

B] 22 equal parts on vernier scale

C] 24 equal parts on vernier scale

D] 25 equal parts on vernier scale

180] Which of the following is not the part of a combination set?

A] Stock

B] Square head

C] Protractor head

D] Centre head

181] The datum, form which the measurements of the vernier height gauge are taken, is...

A] The beam

B] The vernier slide

C] The base

D] Above the scriber poing

vernier height gauge vernier height guage

Vernier Height Gauge

182]The part of a vernier height gauge on which the main scale divisions are graduated is the...

A] Base

B] Beam

C] Fine setting device

D] The vernier plate

183] On which part of the vernier height gauge are the main scale division graduated? ]

A] Base

B] Vernier plate

C] Beam

D] Fine adjusting unit

184] For marking purpose a Vernier height gauge must be on the --------

A] Bed of a machine tool

B] Surface plate

C] Square block

D] Any flat surface

185] Before using Vernier height gauge make sure that the --------

A] Locking screw is in a locked position

B] Scriber is Locked

C] Zero of the vernier coincides with zero of the main scale

D] Gib is Provided

186] The least count Of a vernier height gauge is...........]

A] 0.05 mm

B] 0.1 mm

C] 0.02 mm

D] 0001 mm

187] Which laying out the vernier height gauge must be used on the ----------

A] V block

B] Machine bed

C] Surface plate

D] Any flat surface

188] The part which is slides on the beam of a vernier height gauge is known as a ------

A] Base

B] Beam scale

C] Scriber

D] Vernier slide

189] The base of the vernier height gauge is generally made out of ---------

A] Cast iron]

B] Steel

C] Aluminium alloy

D] Tungsten carbide

190] Which instrument iis used for marking layout?

A] Micrometer

B] Vernier

C] Depth gauge

D] Vernier height gauge

191] While marking with a Vernier height gauge, the work piece is generally ----------

A] Supported by an angle plate

B] Supported by another work piece

C] Held by one hand

D] Held without support

192] Which of the following is not the part of a combination set?

A] Stock

B] Square head

C] Protractor head

D] Centre head

**Engineering Drawing in Mechanical Engineering**

18]The 'T' square is used for drawing lines ......

a] inclined

b] curved

c] vertical

d] horizontal

19] For drawing large size circle is drawn by.....

a] straight bar

b] lengthening bar

c] big bar

d] small bar

20] To draw or measure angle is used by.....

a]set square

b] protractor

c] 'T' square

d] none of these

21] The grade of pencil is used to sketching lettering ........

a] conical point

b] chisel point

c] soft

d] low

22] For drawing thin lines of uniform thickness the pencil should be sharpened in the form of .......

a] chisel edge

b]conical

c] pointed

d] none of these

23] What is used for drawing curves which can not drawn by compass

a] small compass

b] French curve

c] protractor

d] none of these

24]Unnecessary lines is removed by .....

a] Duster

b] sand paper block

c] eraser

d] none of these

25] Circle and arcs are drawn by means of .....l.

a] compass

b] divider

c] lengthening bar

d]none of these

26] Inking pen is used in drawing ......
a] horizontal line
b] non circular arcs
c] vertical lines
d] all of these

27] The card board scale are available in set of .....
a] 7
b] 8
c] 6
d] 9

28] The convenient length size of 30 -60°-90° set square for used in school and colleges are......
a] 250
b] 200
c] 300
d] none of these

29] Drawing board is shape of ........
a] square
b] rectangular
c] triangular
d] none of these

30] The 'T' square , set square ,scale protractor are complain use in.......
a] protractor
b] mini drafter
c] set square
d] none of these

31]Set square , T square edges are bevelled for the purpose of....
a] curve line
b] inking lines
b] taking measurements
d] none of these

32]Geometrical construction which are mostly based on plane geometry and which are very.......
a] Accuracy
b] Quality
c] Essential
d] Superior quality

33] How much method of drawing the regular polygons.......

a] Inscribe circle method and arc method
b] General method for drawing any polygon
c] Alternative method
d] All of these
34] The line AB can be divided into .... equal parts.
a] 7
b] 10
c] 15
d] All of them
35] Which method of constructing triangl in circle......
a] Inscribing
b] Describing
c] Both a and b
d] None of these
36] When two sides of the hexagon are required to be horizontal the starting point for stepping equal division should be on an end of the.....
a] Horizontal diameter
b] Vertical diameter
c] Inclined diameter
d] None of these
37] If two sides of hexagon are required to be vertical the starting point should be on an end of the....
a] Inclined diameter
b] Horizontal diameter
c] Vertical diameter
d] None of these
38] The section obtained by the inter section of the right circular cone by a plane in different position relative to the axis of the cone are called.......
a] Conics
b] Circles
c] Triangles
d] Half circle
39] When the section plane is inclined to the axis and cuts all the generators on one side on a apex the section is in......
a] Conic section
b] Ellipse
c] Parabola
d] Hyperbola

40] When the section plane is inclined to the axis and is parallel to one of the generators the section is a .........

a] Ellipse
b] Parabola
c] Hyperbola
d] Cycloid

41] Use of elliptical curve is........

a] Arches
b] Dams and monuments
c] Manholes, gland & stuffing boxes
d] All of these

42] Use of parabolic curve is.........

a] Bridges & arches
b] Sound reflectors
c] Light reflectors
d] All of these

43] Use of hyperbolical curve is......

a] Cooling towers and water channel
b] Dames
c] Bridges
d] All of these

44] When the point is within the circle, the curve is called an.......

a] Superior trochoid
b] Interior trochoid
c] Trochoid
d] Isotrochoid

45] When the point outside the circle then the curve is called as......

a] Interior trochoid
b] Superior trochoid
c] Trochoid
d] Insuperior trochoid

46] The curve general by a point on a circumference of a circle, which rolls without slipping along another circle it is called.......

a] Epicycloids
b] Hypocycloid
c] Involute
d] None of these

47] When the circle rolls inside another circle the curve is called.......

a] Hypocycloid
b] Epicycloids
c] Trochoid
d] Hypotrochoid
48] The use of archemedian spiral curve is made in........
a] Teeth profiles of helical gears
b] Profiles of cams
c] Both a & b
d] None of these
49] The cams are widely used in........
a] Automates
b] Printing machines
c] C engines
d] All of these
50] Spring index =
a] Diameter of coil / diameter of a wire
b] Diameter of wire /diameter of coil
c] Mean diameter of wire / diameter of coil
d] Mean diameter of a coil / diameter of wire
51] Eccentricity =
a] Distance of a point from the focus / distance of the point from directrix
b] Distance of focus from point / distance of point from
c] Distance of point from focus / distance of directrix of point
d] Distance of point from directrix / distance of point from focus
52] Mathematically an ellipse can be described by equation.....
a] $a^2 / X^2 + y^2 / b^2 = 1$
b] $x^2 / a^2 + y^2 / b^2$
c] $x^2 / a^2 + y^2 / b^2 = 0$
d] $x^2 / a^2 + y^2 / b^2 = 1$
53] Mathematically a parabola can be described by an equation......
a] $y^2 = 4ax$
b] $x^2 = 2ay$
c] $x^2 = 4ay$
d] Both a & b
54] Mathematically hyperbola can be described by an equation.......
a] $x^2 /a^2 - y^2 /b^2 = 1$
b] $x^2 /y^2 - y^2 /x^2 = 0$

c] Both a & b

d] None of these

55] Cycloid can be described by an equation......

a] y = a( 1-cos Ø ]

b] x = a(Ø -sin Ø ]

c] <u>Both a & b</u>

d] None of these

56] The mathematically represented hypocycloid is.....

a] Y = a $\cos^3$ Ø, X = a $\sin^3$ Ø

b] X = a $\sin^3$ Ø, Y = a $\cos^3$ Ø

c] <u>X = a $\cos^3$ Ø, Y = a $\sin^3$ Ø</u>

d] None of these

57] Mathematically represented by involute is

a] X = r sin Ø - r Ø cos Ø, Y = r cos + r Ø sin Ø

b] X = r sin Ø + r cos Ø, Y = r cos Ø – r Ø sin Ø

c] Y = r Ø cos Ø – r sin Ø, X = r sin Ø – r Ø cos Ø

d] <u>X = r cos Ø + r Ø sin Ø, Y =r sin Ø - r Ø cos Ø</u>

58] The lines from the object to the plane are called.......

a] Projection

b] <u>Projector</u>

c] Reference plane

d] None of these

59] The orthographic projection an object is represented by View on the mutual perpendicular projection lines

a] <u>Two or three</u>

b] Three or two

c] Three or four

d] None of these

60] When the projectors are parallel to each other & also perpendicular to the plane, the projection is called......

a] Isometric projection

b] Oblique projection

c] <u>Orthographic projection</u>

d] Perspective projection

61] The two planes employed for the purpose of Orthographic projections are......

a] Auxillary plane

d] Horizontal plane

c] Reference plane

d] None of these

62] The line in which they intersect is termed the reference line & is denoted by the letters.......

a] AB

b] YZ

c] XY

d] None of these

63] The projection on the VP is called........

a] Side view

b] Front view

c] Top view

d] All of these

64] .........Method, when the views are drawn in their relative positions, the plane comes below the elevation. The view of the object as observed from the left-side the right of elevation.

a] Plane of projection

b] First angle projection

c] Third angle projection

d] None of these

65] Third angle projection method, the object is assumed to be situated in the........ quadrant.

a] First quadrant

b] Second quadrant

c] Third quadrant

d] Fourth quadrant

66] .......... Method of projection is used in U.S.A & also in other countries.

a] plane of projection

b] Orthographic projection

c] First-angle projection

d] Third angle projection

67] When an object is situated on the ground, in first angle projection method, the bottom of its ..... will co-inside with XY

a] Top view

b] Front view

c] side view

d] All of these

68] The important element of this projection system

a] An object

b] Plane of projection

c] An observer

d] All of these

69] When line AB is parallel to HP hence .......

a] It' front view to AB

b] It''s side view equal to AB

c] It's top view equal to AB

d] None of these

70] When a line is parallel to a plane; it's projection on plane is equal to it's ;

a] True length

b] True shape

c] True size

d] None of these

71] The point is parallel in which the line or line produced meet the point is plane is called it's .......

a] Line

b] ratio

c] Trace

d] none of these

72] ........ is the shortest distance between two points.

a] a line

b] a point

c] a straight line

d] none of these

73] When the line intersect horizontal plane that's called.....

a] horizontal trace

b] vertical trace

c] trace of line

d] none of these

74]Planes may be divided into two main types ......

a] Perpendicular planes, auxillary planes

b] Perpendicular plane, oblique planes

c] Auxillary planes , perpendicular planes

d] none of these

75] Planes which are inclined to the reference plane are called......

a] Auxillary plane

b] obliqeu plane

c] Perpendicular planes

d] picture plane

76] When a plane is perpendicular to a reference plane it's projection on that plane is a..........

a] horizontal line

b] parallel line

c] straight line

d] none of these

77] When a plane is parallel to a reference plane , it's projection on that plane shows........

a] It's true shape &size

b] It's true length & size

c] It's true height & size

d] none of these

78] Plane perpendicular to VP & HP that plane is called as .........

a] Auxillary Plane

b] Oblique Plane

c] Perpendicular Plane

d] None of these

79] Perpendicular plane can be divides into the following types.........

a] Perpendicular to both the reference planes.

b] Perpendicular to one plane & parallel to other

c] Perpendicular to one plane & inclined to other

d] All of these

80] The planes have only two dimensions, viz........

a] Length & breadth

b] Length & height

c] Length & thickness

d] All of these

81] The imaginary line of prism joining the centrs of the bases called.........

a] Faces

b] Axis

c] Apex

d] Base

82] A right & regular prism has it's axis....... to the bases a] Parallel

b] Perpendicular

c] Inclined

d] None of these

83] When a pyramid or a cone is cut by a plane parallel to it's base thus removing the top portion, the remaining portion is called it's.........

a] Sphere

b] Cone

c] Cylinder

d] Frustum

84] Oblique cylinder & cones have their axes........ to their base

a] Inclined

b] Parallel

c] Perpendicular

d] All of these

85] Projection of two equal sphere s resting on the ground & in contact with each other, with the line joining there centre parallel to the..........

a] A VP

b] VP

c] HP

d] All of these

86] Projections of section on the other plane to which it is inclined is called.......

a] Section planes

b] Apparent section

c] True shape of sphere

d] None of these

87] When the section plane is parallel to the HP or the ground, the true shape of the section will be seen in.........

a] Front view

b] Side view

c] Top view

d] All of these

88] Surface of solid are laid out on a plane the figure obtained is called its........

a] Interpenetration

b] Development

c] Intersection

d] None of these

89] Development of surfaces is essential in.........

a] Foundry shop

b] Sheet metal work

c] Fitting shop

d] None of these

90] Which method of development used in transition pieces?

a] Parallel diameter

b] Radial line method

c] Triangulation method

d] Approximate method

91] Which method of development used in pyramids and cones.........

a] Radial line method

b] Parallel line method

c] Approximate method

d] Triangulation method

92] Parallel line method is used in..........

a] Prism

b] Cylinder

c] Cubes

d] All of these

93] Which method of development used in surface as sphere, paraboloid, ellipsoid, hyperboloid, and helicoids

a] Radial line method

b] Triangulation method

c] Approximate method

d] Parallel line method

94] Zone method and lune method is used in development of........

a] Prisms

b] Cones

c] Sphere

d] Pyramids

95] Calculation the subtended angle $\Theta$ by the formula $\Theta = 360^{0} \times$ radius of the base circle

a] Length of axis

b] Slant height

c] Radius of axis

d] None of these

96] In engineering practice, objects constructed may have constituent part, the surfaces of which intersect one another in lines called........ of intersection.

a] Lines
b] Cones
c] Cylinder
d] Prisms

97] The line of interaction may be depending upon the nature of.......

a] Intersection surface
b] Intersecting solids
c] Intersection cones
d] None of these

98] The two plane surface intersect in a........ line

a] Curve
b] Straight
c] Plane
d] All of these

99] The line of intersection between two curved surface or between......... Surface and a curved surface is a curve.

a] A curved
b] A plane
c] A solids
d] None of these

100] When a solids completely penetration another solids there will be two lines of intersection. These lines are sometimes called the line or........

a] Line of interpenetration
b] Curve of interpenetration
c] Solids of interpenetration
d] All of these

101] Use of penetration curve is.......

a] Sheet metal work
b] Fitting shop
c] Fabricating work
d] Foundry shop

102] Methods of determining the line of intersection between surface of two interpenetration.........

a] Approximate method & radial line method
b] Line method and cutting plane method

c] Triangulation method and parallel line method

d] None of these

103] Example of interpenetration is..........

a] Two prism intersection

b] Cylinder and prism intersection

c] Cone and cylinders intersection

d] <u>All of these</u>

104] Two cylinder intersection is example of.........

a] <u>Intersection</u>

b] Interpenetration

c] Cone intersection

d] None of these

105] ........... Method is explained in detail while solving illustrative problems

a] Line method

b] Radial line method

c] <u>Cutting plane method</u>

d] Parallel line method

106] What is a type of isometric projection?

a] <u>Pictorial projection</u>

b] Orthographic projection

c] Perspective projection

d] Oblique Projection

107] Isometric views have been drawn........

a] Full scale

b] Half scale

c] <u>True length</u>

d] True scale

108] The line parallel to isometric axis are called........

a] Isometric axis

b] <u>Isometric line</u>

c] Isometric planes

d] Isometric views

109] The isometric projection is reduce in the ratio.........

a] 3 :

b] 1 : 2

c] 2 : 2

d] <u>2 : 3</u>

110] The isometric projection of circle drawn with........

a] Isometric Plane

b] Isometric graph

c] Isometric Drawing

d] Isometric Scale

111] The major axis of the ellipse is long than...............

a] Radius of the circle

b] True diameter

c] Diameter of the circle

d] None of these

112] Makes practice for drawing of isometric view using........

a] Isometric planes

b] Isometric lines

c] Isometric graph

d] Isometric view

113] Use of parabolic curve is

a] Sound reflectors

b] Dams

c] Man hole of boiler

d] Gland & stuffing box

114] When the section plane is inclined the true shape of section on

a] AVP

b] VP

c] HP

d] A/P

115] When section plane is perpendicular to both the HP & VP the true shape of section on

a]Top view

b] Side view

c] Front view

d]None of this

116] When view projected on auxiliary planes are called

a] Auxiliary view

b Sectional view

c] Front view

d] None of these

117] Invisible features of an object are shown by means of

a] Outline

b] Chain lines

c] Hidden lines

d] None of these

118] Importance of sectional view on drawing for

a] Internal details

b] Outer details

c] Hatching

d] None of these

119] The component is cut by a straight cutting plane is divided in to two parts

a] Half section

b] Full section

c] Offset section

d] Removed section

120] section line is two different parts (pieces] in contact should be drown in...

a] Same direction

b] Opposite direction

c]parallel direction

d] None of these

121] When area to be sectioned in very small as for this plate and structural members blacked in section may be used. A space of not less than

a] 0.07mm

b] 0.7mm

c] 0.05mm

d] 0.5mm

122] The sum of interior angles of polygon is equal

a] (2*n-4]*Right angle

b] (2*n]*Right angle-4

c] (2*4-n]*Right angle

d] (2-4*n]*Right angle

123] One micron is equal to ..........mm

a] 0.001

b] 1000

c] 0.01

d] 0.1

124] Development of surface is essential in.....

a] foundry shop

b] sheet metal work

c] fitting shop

d] none of these

125] Which method of development used in transition piece?

a] parallel line method

b] radial line method

c] triangulation method

d] none of these

126] The isometric projection is reduced in the ratio of

a] √2:√3

b] √3:√2

c] 1:√2

d] none of these

127] When measurements are required in three units the scale is used....

a] full scale

b] plain scale

c] half scale

d] none of these

128]Isometric drawing is larger in production about isometric projection is....

a] 22.5%

b] 0.815

c] 9/11

d] none of these

129] While isometric of sphere of spherical parts.......is must be used.

a] full scale

b] isometric length

c] true length

d] half scale

130] When circle draw with isometric scale the length of major axis of the ellipse to the ............

a] true diameter

b] isometric diameter

c] isometric diameter

d] none of these

131] In isometric view which contain a large number of non –isometric lines which method is used

a] box method

b] off-set method

c] co-ordinate method

d] centre lay out method

132] When drawing is drawn smaller than actual size of object .....

a] full scale

b] enlarging scale

c] reducing scale

d] none of these

133] When e=1 curve is called.....

a] parabola

b] hyperbola

c] ellipse

d] none of these

134]Compare with isometric drawing the advantage of oblique projection is....

a] front face is in true shape

b] two axis are always perpendicular to each othe

c] receding axis is taken at some convenient angles

d] none of these

135]If all the receding edges are drawn true length the oblique projection is called...

a] cavilier projection

b] cabinet projection

c] general projection

d] none of these

136] The large object such as building the point is usually taken height of .....

a] 0.8mm

b] 1.2mm

c] 1.8mm

d] 1.5mm

137] Central plane is the imaginary vertical plane which passes through....

a] P. P

b] H.L

c] G.P

d] C.P

138] When object is parallel to P.P the perspective is called......

a] one point
b] two point
c] three point
d] none of these

139] The line drawn through the station point from the picture plane shall be ....

a] P.A
b] H.L
c] G.L
d] C

140] The distance of the station point from the picture plane shall be .....

a] Max. Diameter of the object
b] Twice the max. Diameter of the object
c] Half the max. Diameter of the object
d] none of these

141] In isometric view of hexagonal plane all the sides of hexagon is .....

a] equal length
b] unequal length
c] none of these

142] When all the faces are equal & regular the polyhedron is said....

a] regular
b] prisms
c] irregular
d] pyramid

143] Oblique prisms &pyramid have ......

a] axis perpendicular to the base
b] axis inclined to the base
c] faces inclined to the H.P
d] none of these

144] Icosahedrons has equal equilateral triangular faces

a] 12
b] 8
c] 20
d] 6

145] When a pyramid or cone is cut by a plane parallel to its base is called.....

a] pyramid
b] turned carted

c] frustum

d] none of these

146] Plane which are inclined to both the reference plane is called ......

a] oblique plane

b] perpendicular plane

c] inclined plane

d] none of these

147] When a line parallel to H.P & perpendicular to V.P the trace line is.....

a] V.T

b] H.T

c] no trace

d] V.T& H.T

148] When a line parallel to the V.P and inclined to H.P the true length of line in.....

a] front view

b] top view

c] side view

d] none of these

149] When point situated in front quadrant

a] above the H.P & in front of V.P

b] below the H.P & in front of V.P

c] behind the V.P & above H.P

d] below the H.P & behind the V.P

150] Find the quadrant of point "b" is 15 mm above H.P and 25mm behind the V.P

a] I st

b] III rd

c] IIII th

d] II nd

151] In first angle projection front view is ......

a] above the top view

b] below the top view

c] above the side view

d] below the side view

152] In orthographic projection the projectors are ........

a] parallel to plane

b] perpendicular to plane

c] inclined to plane

d] none of these

153] L.H.S.V means.........

a] length of side view

b] left hand view

c] right hand view

d] left hand side view

154] The object lines between the observer and the plane of projection is .......

a] 3rd angle

b] 1st angle

c] 4th angle

d] 2nd angle

155] In third angle projection plane of projection is assumed to be ......

a] non transparent

b] quadrant

c] transparent

d] dihedral angle

156] In third angle projection top view is always on......

a] above front view

b] above top view

c] below the front view

d] below the side view

157] Four quadrants which may be called as......

a] anticlockwise

b] first and third angle

c] dihedral angles

d] none of these

158] In first angle projection method the view see from the left is placed on .....

a] left of the front view

b] right of front view

c] above the top view

d] below the front view

159] The size of A2 paper is .....

a] 297*420

b] 594*841

c] 420*594

d] 210*297

160] The edge of board on which 'T' square is sli9ding is called ......

a] straight edge

b] <u>working edge</u>

c] chisel edge

d] none of these

161] The size of title block as recommended by B.I.S . is .....

a] <u>185*65</u>

b] 150*50

c] 170*65

d] none of these

162] For A2 size sheet the number of zones suggested by B.I.S. along the length & width.......

a] 12,8

b] 16,12

c] 8,6

d] none of these

163] The drawing sheet is so folded that...... is always on the top.

a] drawing

b] lettering

c] title block

d] none of these

164] In free hand sketching horizontal lines are sketched from.......

a] right to left

b] up to down

c] left to right

d] none of these

165] When drawing is down smaller than actual size of object

a] enlarging scale

b] reducing scale

c] full scale

d] none of these

166] The ratio of the length of the object represented on drawing to the actual length of object is called.......

a] full scale

b] R.F.

c] half scale

d] plain scale

167] When measurements are required in three unit the scale is used.....
a] full scale
b] half scale
c] plain scale
d] none of these
168] When protractor is not available the scale of chord is used ......
a] measure length
b] measure angle
c] measure scale
d] none of these
169] The least count of a vernier calliper is ........
a] 0.001
b] 0.02
c] 0.001
d] 0.0002
170] Which scale is used to read a very small unit with great accuracy?
a] plain scale
b] diagonal scale
c] scale of chord
d] vernier scale
171] The R.F. is greater than one (1] the scale is .......
a] plain scale
b] diagonal scale
c] enlarging scale
d] reducing scale

**AutoCAD for Mechanical Engineering**

1] Which is the latest version of AutoCAD software?
a) 2016
b) 2017
c) 2018
d) 2019
2] Which key is used to obtain properties palette in AutoCAD?
a) Control+1
b) Control+2
c) Control+3
d) Control+4
3] AutoCAD was first released in the year:
a) 1858

b) 1966
c) 1898
d) 1982

4] How many units are available in AutoCAD?
a) 4
b) 5
c) 7
d) 6

5] Which mode allows the user to draw 90° straight lines :
a) Osnap
b) Ortho
c) Linear
d) Polar tracking

6] To obtain parallel lines, concentric circles and parallel curves; __________ is used.
a) Array
b) Fillet
c) Copy
d) Offset

7] The default grid spacing in both X and Y directions is:
a) 10
b) 20
c) 5
d) 15

8] How many workspaces are available in AutoCAD?
a) 2
b) 4
c) 3
d) 5

9] Scale command can be accessed easily by typing:
a) SL
b) S
c) SC
d) C

10] Which command is used to divide the object into segments having predefined length?
a) Divide
b) Chamfer

c) Trim

d) Measure

11] How many grip points does a circle have?

a) 5

b) 4

c) 3

d) 2

] When drawing in 2D, what axis do you NOT work with?

A] X

B] Y

C] Z

D] WCS

] The primary difference between the Model tab and the Layout tab(s) is _____.

A] the Model tab is used for drawing in 3D and a Layout is used for drawing in 2D

B] the Model tab is where you create the drawing and a Layout tab represents the sheet that you will plot or print on

C] the color of the background

D] the Model tab displays the drawing you are copying from and the Layout tab is where you lay out the new drawing

] Which of the following is NOT a property of an object

A] Line weight

B] Measure

C] Hyperlink

D] Elevation

] Which command convert discrete objects in polyline

A] Union

B] Subtract

C] Join

D] Polyline

] To print the entire project, you will choose to regulate what to plot

A] Display

B] Extends

C] Limits

D] Window

] What is the usefulness of viewports

A] Allows us to see the screen or on paper different views of the same project

B] Give us the ability to see projects have become a newer version of AutoCAD from our

C] We can make a change in one part of the plan, without affecting the rest

D] None of the above

] What is the difference between the Scale command from the command Zoom

A] Scale for single object, while the Zoom whole plan

B] No difference

C] H Scale can grow / shrink a shape up 10 times, while the Zoom has no limits

D] H Scale changes the size of objects, while the Zoom changes the visibility of the project

] When to fix a block attribute

A] Before you fix the block

B] When I make the block

C] After fix the block

D] No matter the number

] What you cannot create from the command Offset

A] Vertical straight

B] Concentric circles

C] Three parallel lines

D] Parallel arcs

] By what symbol shows the snap point to the closest point

A] with circles and dots in the center

B] With two triangle

C] With three orthogonal

D] With Diamond

] Which state grid is use to design perspective

A] Parametric

B] Isometric

C] Pro-optic

D] Rectangular

] If I want to draw a line in the direction 07:30 (local time) will give an angle

A] -135 degrees

B] 270 degrees

C] -225 degrees

D] None of the above

] When in absolute Cartesian coordinates have points A (10.8) and B (6.5), then to make a line from A -> B with relative polar coordinates will write

A] @ -5 <36.88

B] @ 4 <30

C] @ 5 <216,88

D] @ 3 <60

] What is the minimum allowable number of layers in a drawing

A] 0

B] 5

C] 1

D] 2

] Which of the following is not a keyboard shortcut of AutoCAD?

A] Ctrl + P

B] Alt + F4

C] Ctrl + F4

D] Alt + B

] Why do we have 16,7 M colors in RGB

A] Because so one can distinguish man

B] since this is the limit of graphics cards

C] For each color we have 256 shades and colors combination third

D] Because we want compatibility between PC and Macintosh

] What setting gradient allows us to fill an open area?

A] Gap

B] Tolerance

C] Transparency

D] Open

] What are the various options from left to right and the opposite direction?

A] Choose a different category of objects

B] select objects according to their color

C] Select objects according to their position

D] No difference

] Which is corresponded to zoom mouse wheel?

A] Zoom in / zoom out

B] pan & scan

C] extents / all

D] scale

] What command allows us to select objects based on some status?

A] Properties

B] Qselect

C] Pselect

D] Attributes

] How to make a random line with an angle of 40 degrees to the x axis

A] will write 0 <40

B] will write 2 <40

C] will write 3<40

D] will write 4 <40

] Which of the following file extensions cannot open the AutoCAD

A] dwg

B] dxf

C] dot

D] dws

] A surveyor with a headband to measure the dimensions of a site, he make measurements by

A] No one method

B] Related Cartesian coordinates

C] Absolute polar coordinates

D] None of the above

] What is the command used for Plagiostomi angle?

A] Chamfer

B] Fillet

C] Offset

D] Mirror

] When should I use the Block Editor

A] To write text block

B] To fix outer block

C] To fix dynamic block

D] To store it in another version of AutoCAD

] If the scheme that stores will be opened in AutoCAD 2006 then you must save it in

A] AutoCAD 2004 dwg

B] AutoCAD 2006 dwg

C] AutoCAD 2007 dwg
D] None of the above
] Print scale 1:50 means that
A] The draft is 50 times less expensive than the original
B] A 3 cm corresponds to half a meter
C] A measure corresponds to 50 cm
D] None of the above
29] What do the letters UCS
A] Uniform Calculator System
B] United CAD System
C] Universal CAD Settings
D] Universal Coordinate System

] What is the difference of two regular 8-gonon, which is one inscribed and another circumscribed circle
A] No difference
B] different opening angles
C] different side length
D] different crowd sides

] If during the CCW measurement result gives an angle 135 degrees, the same CW angle measured is
A] 225 degrees
B] -135 degrees
C] -225 degrees
D] 135 degrees

] What does associative hatch
A] Monitors the changes in shape that fills
B] Relates to the other hatch plan
C] Both of the above
D] None of the above

] What is the difference between command Plot and Print
A] plot command prints only big plans
B] The plot command for CNC (CAM)
C] No difference
D] print command can print up to A3 size paper

] If you change the scale list a project that I have started from 1:50 1:10 then

A] You will have to start over

B] You should not raise the objects already exist (scale) by 5

C] You will not need to change anything in hitherto methodology

D] should be converted into new items that will add based on the new scale

] Which of the following is NOT a unit of length measurement?

A] Yards

B] Parsecs

C] Microns

D] Grads

] What does the command Wblock

A] Warp-speed block

B] Write block

C] Window block

D] Wide-area block

] Where should you pay attention when you are working with autocad commands?

A] Drawing area

B] Status bar

C] Tool bars

D] Command window

] Polar coordinates are used mostly for drawing______

A] Arc

B] Ellipse

C] Angular lines

D] None of the above

] How many SNAP points does an object have?

A] 1

B] 4

C] 5

D] Depend on object

] How many points do you need to define for the rectangle command?

A] One

B] Two

C] Three

D] Four

] How many AutoCAD objects are in a rectangle?

A] One

B] Two

C] Three

D] Four

] How will you deselect an object while you are selecting set of objects?

A] Ctrl+ click on the object to be removed

B] Shift + Click on the object to be removed

C] Alt + Click on the object to be removed

D] None of the above

] How long will a line from 0,5 to 5,5 be ________

A] 10 units

B] 5 units

C] 15 units

D] None of the above

] Objects are rotated around the

A] Bottom of the object

B] Base point

C] Center of the object

D] Origin

] The origin of a drawing is at

A] 0,0

B] 1,0

C] 0,1

D] 1,1

] How would you select set of objects in a drawing?

A] By a crossing window drawn from right to left

B] By a crossing window drawn left to right

C] Shift+ clicking on the objects

D] None of the above

] Fillet command can be used to obtain__________
A] Sharp corners
B] Round corners
C] Both of the above
D] None of the above

] A polar array creates new objects_____
A] In a grid pattern
B] In a circular pattern
C] In a straight line
D] All of the above

] How many layers a drawing should have?
A] 1
B] 2
C] As many as depending on the complexity
D] None of the above

] Scaling objects make them_______
A] Smaller
B] Bigger
C] Either smaller or bigger
D] None of the above

**Electrical MCQ for Mechanical Engineering**

85] A heater draws a current of 8A when connected to a 240V source] What is the resistance value of the heater element in ohms?
A] 40
B] 20
C] 30
D] 60

86] An electric soldering iron with an 80 ohms heating element is plugged into a 240V outlet] How much current will be drawn by the iron?
A] 2A
B] 3A
C] 4A
D] 5A

87] The alternator in a car delivers 4A and has a load of 3 ohms connected across its terminals] Find the voltage of the circuit

A] 18V

B] 24V

C] <u>12V</u>

D] 16V

88] Three resistors of 1K ohms, 2K ohms and 7K ohms are connected in series with a 30 V supply] If 2 K ohms and 7 K ohms resistors are open circuited, a voltmeter connected across the 7K ohms resistor will indicate...

A] 10 k ohms, 3A

B] 10 k ohms, 300mA

C] <u>10 k ohms, 3 mA</u>

D] 5 k ohms, 6 mA

89] A voltage source produces an IR drop of 40V across a 20 ohms resistance, 60V across a 30 ohms resistance and 180V across a 90 ohms resistance all in series] How much is the applied voltage?

A] 180 V

B] 240 V

C] 100 V

D] <u>280 V</u>

90] Three resistors 27 ohms, 47 ohms and 68 ohms are connected in parallel] What is the otal resistance?

A] <u>less than 27 ohms</u>

B] greater than 68 ohms

C] between 27 and 47 ohms

D] sum of all the three resistances

91] One million and one mege ohms resistors are there if connected both in parallel, what would be the combined resistance value?

A] <u>0.5 mega ohm</u>

B] 0.5 milli ohm

C] 0.5 kilo ohm

D] 0.5 ohm

92] A 24 ohms and a 8 ohms resistors in parallel gets a combined resistance of...

A] <u>6 ohms</u>

B] 12 ohms

C] 3 ohms

D] 32 ohms

93] Resistors of the following values are connected in parallel, 5 ohms, 5 kilo-ohms, 50 kilo-ohms, 5 mega ohms] Their equivalent resistance will be very near to...

A] 4.5 ohms

B] 4500 ohms

C] 45000 ohms

D] 4,500,000 ohms

94] The resistance of given wire is 2 ohms] The resistance of the other wire made of the same material having twice the length and twice the cross sectional area is...

A] 5 ohms

B] 6 ohms

C] 2 ohms

D] 8 ohms

95] If the area of a metal wire of a given length is doubles, its resistance will...

A] be doubled

B] be halved

C] remain the same

D] be four times more

96].Among the following only one is regarded as resistance wire

A] gold

B] silver

C] nichrome

D] copper

97] Arc heating occurs when the air between electrodes of opposite polarity becomes..

A] moistened

B] dry

C] ionized

D] none of the above

98] The meter used to measure the temperature of furnace is...

A] hydrometer

B] pyrometer

C] hygrometer

D] tachometer

99] in the case of electrolyte a rise in temperature causes...

A] decrease in resistance

B] increase in resistance

C] no change in resistance

D] none of the above

100] Heat developed in a conductor is proportional to the...

A] square of the power

B] square of the resistance

C] square of the current

D] square of the time

101] Out of the four metal/alloys given below, one has almost no change in resistance for temperature change...

A] nickel

B] nichrome

C] platinum

D] manganin

102] A material that is slightly repelled by a magnet is called ...

A] magnetic

B] paramagnetic

C] diamagnetic

D] ferromagnetic

103] A material that can be magnetized only very slightly is called...

A] magnetic

B] paramagnetic

C] diamagnetic

D] ferromagnetic

104] Substances that can be magnetized easily and make very strong magnets are called...

A] ferromagnetic

B] diamagnetic

C] paramagnetic

D] permanent magnetic

105] A substance that has a high retentivity can be used for the manufacture of...

A] electromagnets

B] permanent magnets

C] temporary magnets

D] paramagnets

106] A substance that has low retentivity can be used for the manufacture of...

A] electromagnets
B] permanent magnets
C] bar magnets
D] paramagnets
107] The symbol for inductance is...
A] H
B] I
C] L
D] X
108] Tube lamp choke is the best example of...
A] open circuited
B] short circuited
C] grounded
D] connected to the neutral line
109] The initial function of a choke in a tube light circuit is to...
A] limit the starting current
B] induce high voltage
C] heat up the filament
D] limit the current after starting
110] The second function of a choke in a tube light circuit is to...
A] limit the starting current
B] induce high voltage
C] heat up the filament
D] limit the current after starting
111] The periodic time of a wave from is 2ms] Calculate the frequency
A] 50 HZ
B] 5 HZ
C] 500HZ
D] 5 KHZ
112] How big is the peak amplitude of a sine-wave with an effective value of 220 volts?
A] 311 V
B] 380 V
C] 400 V
D] 440 V
113] The peak-to-peak voltage is 99V] how big is the effective value of the sine wave?
A] 70 V

B] 44.5V

C] 49.5 V

D] 35 V

114] A moving coil voltmeter reads 10 V AC] How big is the effective voltage?

A] higher

B] lower

C] the same

D] 10% higher

115] A moving iron ammeter reads 10 A] how big is the peak current of the oscillation?

A] 7.07 A

B] 1.1414A

C] 70.7 A

D] 14.1 A

116] A current of 2 amps flows through a resistance of 10 ohms] The power dissipated in the resistance is equal to...

A] 20 watts

B] 200 watts

C] 40 watts

D] 5 watts

117] If the frequency changes from 50 HZ to 100 HZ keeping voltage constant, the inductive reactance of coil connected to supply...

A] remains same

B] become half

C] become doubled

D] become 4 times

118] Capacitance is not affected by...

A] plate area

B] distance between plates

C] dialectic material

D] frequency

119] The capacitive reactance of a capacitor varies...

A] directly with frequency

B] inversely with frequency

C] directly with applied voltage

D] inversely with applied voltage

120] A capacitor acquired 3 coulombs of charge when 6 volts are applied across it] It has a capacitance of ...

A] 0.5 farad

B] 3 farads

C] 3 farads

D] 18 farads

121] A capacitor is connected across a 200 volt AC line, its minimum voltage rating should be...

A] 100 volts

B] 200 Volts

C] 300 volts

D] 400 volts

122] when testing a capacitor with an ohmmeter, the meter indicates some resistance] The capacitor under test is...

A] leaky

B] open

C] good

D] short

123] The total capacitance of a 40 micro farad capacitor connected in series with an 80 micro farad capacitor is...

A] 26.7 micro farad

B] 40 micro farad

C] 60.6 micro farad

D] 120 micro farad

124] For obtaining 1 micro farad capacitor from 3 nos] of 3 micro farad capacitors we have to connect...

A] all in parallel

B] all in series

C] 2 series and one in parallel

D] none of the above

125] In an AC series circuit having R and C the current flowing through the capacitor will be...

A] lagging the voltage

B] leading the voltage

C] in phase with the voltage

D] none of the above

126] If the frequency of the supply is increased in the R-C series circuit the capacitive reactance will be

A] reduced
B] increased
C] having no effect
D] none of the above
127] Power companies are interested in improving the power factor to
A] reduce line current
B] increase motor efficiency
C] increase volt-amperes
D] decrease power
128] A capacitor increases the power factor value of an AC motor load when it is connected...
A] in series with the motor
B] in series with the starter
C] in parallel with the motor
D] in series with the main winding
129] Normally, the power factor of an incandescent lighting circuit is..
A] 0
B] 0.5
C] 0.707
D] 1.0
130] When resistance alone is used to determine current in an RLC series circuit, the circuit is...
A] an inductive circuit
B] a capacitive circuit
C] a combination circuit
D] a resonant circuit
131] Inductive reactance is directly related to..
A] resistance
B] frequency
C] capacitance
D] power
132] Synchronous motor when used for power factor improvement should be...
A] under excited
B] over excited
C] loaded
D] running at no load
133] In a RL parallel circuit, the opposition to total current is called...

A] reactance
B] resistance
C] a vector sum
D] impedance
134] In a AC parallel RL circuit, the power dissipated at the
A] impedance
B] resistance
C] inductance
D] capacitance
135] How much is the nominal output voltage of a carbon zinc cell?
A] 12V
B] 1.5V
C] 2.0V
D] 2.2V
136] Cells are connected in series to..
A] increase the output voltage
B] decreases the output voltage
C] decrease the internal resistance
D] increase the current capacity
54137connected in
A] series
B] parallel
C] series-parallel
D] parallel-series
138] The capacity of a cell is measured in
A] watt-hour
B] watts
C] amperes
D] ampere-hour
139] The primary cell which has the shortest shelf life is
A] carbon – zinc
B] alkaline
C] mercury
D] lithium
140] The cell which has very high energy density for given weight or volume to
A] carbon-zinc
B] alkaline

C] mercury

D] lithium

141] A 100-Ah capacity battery should deliver a current of 8A for approximately...

A] 12 h

B] 8 h

C] 20 h

D] 100 h

142] When the battery is needed to be kept idle for a long time...

A] overcharge the battery

B] remove electrolyte

C] clean the plates with distilled water

D] dry them and store the battery in cool dry clean place

143] The active materials of the nickel iron cell are...

A] nickel hydroxide

B] powdered iron and its oxide

C] 21% solution of caustic potash

D] all the above materials

144] The capacity of a cell is measured in

A] watt hour

B] watts

C] amperes

D] ampere-hour

145] To charge a secondary cell, the system used is

A] low voltage AC

B] high voltage AC

C] AC

D] DC

146] What is the number of phases in a normal industrial supply system?

A] one

B] three

C] four

D] two

147] In a 3 phase star connected alternator, the coils have a phase difference of...

A] 120°

B] 240°

C] 60°

D] 360◦

148] Delta connection is used no one of the following

A] primary of the transmission line transformer

B] alternator winding

C] secondary of the distribution transformer

D] primary of the distribution transformer

149] Which method can be used to measure the power in a 3-phase unbalanced load system?

A] one wattmeter method

B] tow wattmeter method

C] three wattmeter method

D] three ammeter method

150] Two wattmeters can be used to measure 3-hase power in a 3-phase, 3 wire system with...

A] balanced load

B] unbalanced load

C] balanced as well as unbalanced load

D] out of balanced load

151] A single wattmeter can be used to measure power in a 3-phase system only when the load is..

A] balanaced

B] unbalanced

C] balanced as well as unbalanced load

D] constant

152] The force producing movement of the pointer in an indicating instrument is called as...

A] deflecting force

B] controlling force

C] damping force

D] distracting force

153] A permanent magnet moving coil instrument will read...

A] only AC quantities

B] only DC quantities

C] both AC and DC quantities

D] pulsating quantities

154] An instrument using gravity control will read correctly if used in..

A] vertical position only

B] horizontal position only

C] inclined position only

D] any position

155] Which one of the following damping methods is used in permanent magnet moving coil instrument?

A] air damping

B] fluid damping

C] spring damping

D] eddy current damping

156] Moving coil instrument works on the effect of...

A] chemical effect

B] heating effect

C] electrostatic effect

D] electromagnetic effect

157] The meter installed at your house to measure electrical energy is an example of...

A] indication type instrument

B] recording type instrument

C] indicating as well as recording type instrument

D] integrating type instrument

158].Which of the following material is preferred for permanent magnet?

A] alnico

B] y-alloy

C] silicon steel

D] wrought iron

159] The instrument which could be classified as absolute instrument is...

A] milli ammeter

B] micro ammeter

C] galvanometer

D] tangent galvanomer

160] Which of the following methods of damping is commonly used in moving iron instrument?

A] Air damping

B] fluid damping

C] eddy current damping

D] viscosity damping

161] The deflecting torque of a moving iron instrument is directly proportional to the..

A] current

B] <u>square of the current</u>

C] square root of the current

D] voltage

162]Which of the following is used for measuring the medium resistance directly?

A] ammeter

B] <u>megger</u>

C] ohmmeter

D] voltmeter

163] An ohmmeter is used for measuring the...

A] insulation resistance

B] <u>resistance</u>

C] currcnt

D] potential difference

164] Which of the following components is not a part of an ohmmeter?

A] fixed resistor

B] variable resistor

C] <u>capacitor</u>

D] battery

165] In shunt ohmmeter, maximum deflection signifies ..

A] <u>maximum resistance</u>

B] minimum resistance

C] a fault in the megger

D] none of these

166].An unknown DC voltage is to be measured, which measuring range will you select first?

A] <u>500V</u>

B] 50V

C] 1.5 V

D] 0.5V

167].An unknown direct current of micro ampere rating is to be measured, which measuring range will you select first?

A] 20 micro amp

B] 15 micro amp

C] 150 micro amp

D] 500 micro amp

168] A multimeter cannot measure...

A] current

B] potential difference

C] capacitance

D] resistance

169] Dynamometer type meters are used to measure...

A] only AC quantities

B] only DC quantities

C] both AC and DC

D] pulsating AC only

170] Which effect is used in wattmeter?

A] electrodynamic effect

B] thermal effect

C] chemical effect

D] electrostatic effect

171] Which of the instrument listed below operates efficiently as wattmeter in both AC and DC?

A] PMMC instrument

B] dynamometer instrument

C] hot wire instrument

D] MI instrument

172] Electrodynamic type of instrument are used commonly for the measurement of...

A] voltage

B] current

C] resistance D]

173] When the phase and neutral of the energy meter are interchanged, its disc...

A] rotates in reverse direction

B ] rotates in correct direction

C] will stop

D] rotates slowly

E] rotates at high speed

174] When the disc of energy meter is rotating even without connecting any load, the error is called

A] creeping error

B] phase error

C] friction error

D] temperature error

175] AC single phase energy meters record the energy in the unit of...

A] kilowatt hours

B] number of thousands of disc rotation

C] volt amperes

D] kilo volt ampere

176] A megger measures resistance in...

A] ohms

B] hundreds of ohms

C] thousands of ohms

D] millions of ohms

177] A megger is exclusively designed for measuring..

A] very high resistance

B] very low resistance

C] ground faults in power lines

D] over loads on DC motors

178] For pipe earthing the minimum internal diameter of galvanized iron of steel pipe required is...

A] 12.5 mm

B] 16mm

C] 3.5 mm

D] 4 m

179] The earth conductor provides a path to ground for..

A] leakage current

B] over current

C] high voltage

D] circuit current

180] if the size of the circuit copper conductor is 10 sq-mm then the size of earth conductor in G.I] wire should be...

A] 1.5 sq.mm

B] 2.5 sq.mm

C] 5 sq.mm

D] 10 sq.mm

181] One calory is equal to,,,

A] 4187 joules

B] 418.7 joules

C] 41.87 joules

D] 4.187 joules

182] The operating temperature range of electrical stove with bare heating element is...

A] 300◦ to 400◦C

B] 500◦ to 600◦C

C] 550◦ to 900◦C

D] 1100◦ to 1300◦C

183] Which appliance works on heating effect of electric current?

A] incandescent lamp

B] bimetallic thermostat

C] H R C fuse

D] toaster

184] What is the size of nichrome wire for heating element of 1000 watts, 230V heater at 500◦C?

A] 18 SWG

B] 20SWG

C] 24 SWG

D] 25 SWG

185] The heat proof insulating material used for heater base is...

A] mica

B] porcelain

C] asbestos

D] glass wool

186].The temperature regulating component of an automatic electric iron is...

A] heating element

B] thermostat

C] sole plate

D] pressure plate

187].The bread toasting zone temperature is about...

A] 400◦C

B] 800◦C

C] 260◦C

D] 975◦C

188] If a winding makes electrical contact with the metal case of the mixer motor the winding is...

A] grounded

B] open circuited

C] short circuited

D] loose connected

189] If the end shafts of a rotor turns blue it is an indication of...

A] scoring

B] overheating

C] freezing

D] burring

190] What type of motor is used in a food mixer?

A] DC shunt motor

B] universal motor

C] capacitor start motor

D] capacitor start and run motor

191] In what position is the motor mounted in most of the mixers?

A] vertical

B] horizontal

C] inclined

D] parallel

**CNC Machining MCQ for Mechanical Engineering**

CNC Machine Tape Punch

image

248] Tape punch having 1 inch in width tape it is made by

A] Paper Mylar

B] Aluminum Mylar

C] Plastic

D] Above all

249] In point two point positioning positioning system........] Is acceptable

A] Open loop control system

B] Closed loop control system

C] Above both

D] None of them

250] In CNC machine having.......

A] Lead screw

B] Ball lead screw

C] Above both

D] None of both

CNC Program Coordinate

image

251] The aim of sub program is........

A] For find coordinates X Y Z.

B] For other small machine.

C] To avoid cutting tool nose tool nose penetration in Jobs surface of high speed.

D] While machining of job in special condition do not use time to time of program block.

252] What is mean by while while xyz co-ordinate point measure zero-measurement

A] Reference mark.

B] Work zero

C] Co-ordinate points

D] Above all

253] CNC machine specified by axis......

A] 2 axis

B] 3 axis

C] 4 axis

D] Above all

CNC Machine Axis

image

254] Xyz axis of CNC machines which point is used for measurements.
A] Work zero point
B] Machine zero point
C] Common zero point
D] Above all
255] Following which point is not useful in CNC machine.
A] various operation done on CNC machine.
B] Less amount for inspection.
C] Hard for setting measure.
D] Machine efficiency is depend upon operators skill.
256] For selection of zero offset before necessary..........
A] cutter is fixed on machine table.
B] The data entered in machine.
C] Job is fixed on machine table.
D] Speed and feed selection necessary before machine operates.
CNC Work Zero Offset Setting.

image

257] In zero offset program indicates........] Code of following
A] X y z
B] X0 y0 z00
C] X10 Y20 Z30

D] G71

258] Work zero is

A] Datum of machine zero on job position.

B] Indicate by X0Y0Z0.

C] Selection of point on job according to program.

D] The end of machining point

259] M command is used for starting operation and complete revolution cycle M03 means.

A] Stop the program.

B] Program completed and reset.

C] Complete the program.

D] Spindle clockwise motion.

CNC Machine Power Pack

image

260] CNC machine is not manually operated it is control by...........

A] Program

B] operation

C] Cam

D] Plug board system

261] In CNC machine M13 means

A] coolant stop

B] coolant on

C] spindle stop

D] coolant on & spindle on

262] The function of power pack in CNC machine.

A] For balancing of lubricants heat.

B] For increasing heat of lubricants.

C] For destroy heat of lubricant.

D] Above all.

CNC Machine Bed.

image

263] The section of CNC machine bed is.....

A] Flat

B] Half round

C] Rectangular

D] Triangular

264] Following which statement is disadvantage of CNC machine.

A] Less inspection charge.

B] Less tooling charge.

C] Increase production rate.

D] High establishment charge.

265] The point to point system is more effective for......

A] Turning

B] Profile milling

C] Grinding

D] Drilling

Tool Setting on NC Machine.

image

266] Tool setting on NC machine on......] unit.

A] Presetting device.

B] Order special device without machine.

C] On n c machine other empty time.

D] When other operation working on machine.

267] For measuring system having built-in coordinates in this system..........] is called zero position.

A] Reference point.

B] Machine zero point.

C] Work zero point

D] Program zero point.

268] Job turning on CNC machine 50 mm dia turn with programs said the trial run 50.1 mm at production time following which Idea used for correct dia making

A] by increase offset of tool 0.1 mm.

B] by increase offset of tool 0.05 mm

C] by decrease offset of tool 0.05 mm

D] by decrease offset of tool 0.1 mm

CNC Copying Lathe Machine.

image

269] For measure zero offset dim dimensions on CNC machine.........mode is set

A] MDI

B] Jog

C] Automatic

D] preset

270] Coping unit of copying lathe is work on

A] Mechanical power system

B] Hand power system

C] Hydraulic power system

D] None of them

271] Following which advantage of Pneumatic power system

A] For increase production rate.

B] Less cash for layout

C] Good climate for work

D] Above all

Principle of CNC Machine Templates.

image

272] For face copying........] Type template is used

A] Rounded

B] Plate type

C] Flat

D] Triangular

273]............] Is Main principle of CNC MACHINE?

A] Indicate all states in numbers

B] More time required for mechanical control on machine.

C] Cutting speed is more than manual control.

D] Production sequence in workshop is stored by block number in machine.

274] For copy of one shaft.......] Type template is used.

A] Rounded

B] Triangular

C] Flats

D] Square

CNC Program Tool Path.

image

275] The symptoms of continuous path is

A] Called counting system.

B] Tool and work piece on co-ordinate Axis for inter related motion.

C] By the setting of cutter feed and speed

D] Above all

276] Misc command M30 means........

A] End of program and reset

B] Program stop

C] Clockwise motion of spindle

D] Complete the programs

277] Following which affect on milling surface while by milling with unsetting spindle vertical milling machine with- longitudinal feed.

A] Convex surface

B] Concave surface

C] Radius cross line

D] Rough surface

CNC Milling Operation]

image

278] While milling by vertical milling machine with 12 mm dia end mill cutter through slot provide on mild steel plate the cutter is sleep and broken for this fault how it is avoid.

A] High speed spindle

B] Low cutting speed

C] Increase of cut depth

D] Less the depth and feed of cutter

279] Having 5 mm pitch of screw and dividing ratio of 40 : 1 what is lead of milling machine

A] 0.25 mm

B] 5 mm

C] 8 mm

D] 200 mm

280] If not use of backlash Eliminator slap cutter used for down milling operation which safety to be observed?

A] Less lead and depth

B] High lead

C] high lead and less depth

D] High lead and high speed

CNC Machine Zero & Feed Rate.

cnc machine zero.PNG

281] Zero offset is the distance between.....] And.........

A] G41 & g42

B] Machine zero & work zero

C] Reference point and tapping mode

D] None of them

282] The feed rate is programmed as mm per minute with G .........] And mm per- Revolution with G.

A] G41 & g42

B] G 43 and G 40

C] G 94 and g95

D] None of them

283] For collection all instructions from.......] In CNC control unit

A] Memory

B] Tape reader

C] Control panel

D] Operator

CNC Drilling Machine.

cnc drilling machine.jpg

284] For control forward and backward of- CNC drilling machine y axis.........

A] Spindle

B] Table

C] Clockwise

D] Column

285] M 01 command means.....

A] For stopping programs

B] End of program and reset

C] Stopping programs condition

D] Clockwise rotation of machine spindle

286] CNC machine is founded by American scientist john person in.......] Year

A] 1950

B] 1952

C] 1955

D] 1957

CNC Control, Input & Memory Unit.

cnc control.jpg

287] Name of unit used to command the CNC machine.

A] Control unit

B] Memory unit

C] Input unit

D] Output unit

288] Name of unit used to processing the data in CNC machine.

A] Memory unit

B] Control unit

C] Input unit

D] Output unit

289] Name of unit used to storing the data in CNC machine.

A] Input unit

B] Control unit

C] Memory unit

D] Output unit

Servo Motor in CNC Machine.

servo motor.jpg

290] Name of unit used to calculation of data in CNC machine.

A] Output unit

B] Arithmetic unit

C] Memory unit

D] Input unit

291] Name of unit used to display result of processing data in CNC machine

A] Arithmetic unit

B] Output unit

C] Memory unit

D] Input unit

292] Servo Motor in CNC machine is used to.............

A] Changing tool on machine spindle

B] Driving machine spindle

C] Fixing job on machine spindle

D] Proving job on spindle

Types of CNC Machine.

types of cnc.jpg

293] One of the below part of CNC machine used to changing tools on spindle.

A] Servo Motor

B] Control panel

C] Automatic tool changer A T C

D] High speed spindle

294] One of the below CNC machine in CNC milling category is.......

A] Chucking centre

B] CNC late

C] Vertical machining centre

D] Surface grinding machine

295] One of the below CNC machine in turning centre or CNC lathe category is.......

A] Vertical machining centre

B] Horizontal machining centre

C] Vertical turning centre

D] Profile grinding machine

Miscellaneous Functions for CNC Machine.

miscellaneous function.jpg

296] One of the below CNC machine in grinding Centre category is.....

A] Universal milling centre

B] Cylindrical grinding machine
C] CNC late
D] Vertical machining centre

Grinding wheels 1 grinding wheel

Grinding

297] In CNC Machine programming word M indicates
A] Feed rate
B] Spindle speed
C] Miscellaneous function
D] Tool number

298] In CNC Machine programming preparatory function G00 is for.....
A] Linear interpolation
B] Clockwise circular interpolation
C] Counter clockwise circular interpellation
D] Hold

Preparatory Functions for CNC Machine.

preparatory function.jpg

299] In CNC Machine programming preparatory function G02 is for.....
A] Linear interpolation
B] Clockwise circular interpolation
C] Counter clockwise circular interpellation

D] Hold

300] One of the bellow preparatory function G 00 is used in CNC program for.........

A] Linear interpellation or feed motion in straight line.

B] Clockwise circular interpellation

C] Point to point Positioning or Rapid motion.

D] Counter clockwise circular interpellation

301] One of the bellow preparatory function used in CNC program for 3D interpellation

A] G 05

B] G12

C] G17

D] G18

Threading & Tapping on CNC Machine.

threading & tapping on cnc.jpg

302] One of the bellow preparatory you function used in CNC program for thread cutting constant lead

A] G33

B] G40

C] G53

D] G62

303] One of the bellow preparatory function used in CNC program for tapping operation.

A] G-40

B] G53

C] G62

D] G63

304] One of the below preparatory function used in CNC program for milling operation.

A] G62

B] G63

C] G 78, 79

D] G81

Drilling, Boring & Reaming on CNC Machine

drilling boring & reaming.jpg

305] One of the bellow preparatory function used in CNC program for drilling operation.

A] G 81

B] G 82

C] G 84

D] G 85

306] One of the bellow preparatory function used in CNC program for reaming operation.

A] G 84

B] G 85

C] G 86

D] G 90

307] One of the below preparatory function used in CNC program for boring operation.

A] G 86

B] G 90

C] G 91

D] G 92

CNC Program Sequence Number.

cnc program sequence.png

308] In CNC program which letter is used to indicate the sequence number of the block

A] N

B] G

C] F

D] S

309] In CNC program which letter is used to indicate position of linear axis

A] ABC

B] UVW

C] XYZ

D] IJK

310] One of the below letters used in CNC program for Feed rate

A] S

B] F

C] T

D] M

Tool Change & Spindle Speed in CNC Machine.

tool change i cnc.jpg

311] One of the below letters used in CNC program for spindle speed in RPM

A] M

B] T

C] S

D] F

312] In CNC program which letter is used to indicate TOOL function number of tool

A] T

B] S

C] M

D] F

313] In CNC program which miscellaneous function used to program stop

A] M03

B] M00

C] M01

D] M02

CNC Machine Spindle Direction.

cnc machine spindle direction.png

314] One of the below miscellaneous function used to program optional Stop

A] M 01

B] M 02

C] M 03

D] M 04

315] In CNC program miscellaneous function M02 is used to......

A] Program stop

B] Optional program stop

C] End of program

D] Clockwise spindle on

316] In CNC program miscellaneous function M03 is used to..........

A] Counter clockwise spindle on

B] Clockwise spindle on

C] Spindle off

D] Tool change

Coolant in CNC Machine.

coolant in cnc machine.jpg

317] One of the below miscellaneous function used in CNC program for spindle stop.

A] M04

B] M05

C] M06

D] M07

318] In CNC program which miscellaneous function is used for Tools change

A] M06

B] M07

C] M09

D] M10

319] One of the below miscellaneous function used in CNC program for coolant on

A] M08

B] M09

C] M10

D] M11

Clamping the Job on CNC Machine.

clamping the job on cnc.jpg

320] One of the below miscellaneous function in CNC program used for coolant off

A] M11

B] M10

C] M9

D] M15

321] In CNC program which miscellaneous function used for clamping the job on machine table.

A] M09

B] M10

C] M11

D] M15

322] One of the below miscellaneous function in CNC program used for unclamp the job

A] M11

B] M15

C] M30

D] M60

Work piece change in CNC Machine.

workpice change in cnc.jpg

323] In CNC program which miscellaneous function used for change of workpiece

A] M30

B] M60

C] M68

D] M78

324] The machine is.........for zero off-setting on CNC Machine.

A] In MDI Mode

B] In JOG Mode

C] In Automatic Mode

D] In Present Mode

325] The feed rate on NC Machine is indicate by ......code.

A] X

B] Y

C] F

D] Z

CNC Machine Axis Position]

cnc machine axis position.jpg

326] The position of axis is indicate by.......code.

A] X,Y,Z

B] P,Q,R

C] A,B,C

D] M,N,O

327] CNC Drilling Machine is on.......Axis Programmed.

A] Two Axis

B] Three Axis

C] Four Axis

D] Six Axis

328] From.......unit collect instruction in control unit of CNC

A] Machine Tool

B] Instruction

C] Magnetic Box

D] Memory

Working Graph of CNC Machine]

working graph of cnc machine.jpg

329] For preparing tape of NC Machine----------code is used.

A] EIA Code

B] ISO Code

C] ASC Code

D] None of them.

330] CNC Machine gives more accurate production than convention machine, But it is more expensive because.

A] It has AC cabin

B] It has dust proof cabin

C] It has strong foundation

D] It has more space

331] CNC Machine is working on graphical base the point on digital line, indicated digital points call..........

A] Graph

B] Input Media

C] Co-Ordinate

D] Original Point

Axis Rotary Motion in CNC Machine]

axis rotary motion in CNC.png

332] On CNC Machine for longitudinal feed has.......axes, cross feed......axis and for vertical feed........axis name given.

A] A,B,C

B] X,Y,Z

C] P,Q,R

D] M,N,O

333] For rotary motion CNC machine axis has.......name given.

A] A,B,C

B] X,Y,Z

C] P,Q,R
D] M,N,O
334] CNC Machine means.......
A] Natural Control Machine
B] Pneumatic control Machine
C] Numerical Control Machine
D] No Command Machine

**Engineering Physics MCQ for Mechanical Engineering**

1. Which one of the following is the property of an ionic compound?
a) High melting and boiling points
b) Low melting and boiling points
c) Weak inter-atomic forces
d) Non conductors of electricity
2. When do ionic compounds conduct electricity?
a) In gaseous state
b) In solid state
c) When dissolved in water
d) They never conduct
3. Which of the following covalent compounds conduct electricity?
a) Silica
b) Graphite
c) Diamond
d) Hydrogen chloride
4. Which of the following is a crystalline solid?
a) Anisotropic substances
b) Isotropic substances
c) Supercooled liquids
d) Amorphous solids
5. Why are the glasses of building milky?
a) Because of unwanted deposits
b) Because it becomes old
c) Because it is brittle
d) Because it changes in properties
6. Which of the following has body centered cubic structure?
a) Polonium
b) Copper
c) Nickel
d) Tungsten

7. What is the possible number of different types of lattices (3D)?
a) 4
b) 8
c) 14
d) 17

8. What is the lattice constant for FCC crystal having atomic radius 1.476 Å
a) 1.476 Å
b) 4.1748 Å
c) 5.216 Å
d) 0

9. The interplanar spacing of (220) planes of a FCC structure is 1.7458 Å. Calculate the lattice constant.
a) 4.983 Å
b) 2.458 Å
c) 0
d) 5.125 Å

10. Iron has a BCC structure with atomic radius 0.123 Å. Find the lattice constant.
a) 0
b) 4.587 Å
c) 2.314 Å
d) 0.2840 Å

11. Which of the following is true about the universe?
a) It is an open system
b) It is a closed system
c) It is an isolated system
d) It is an international system

12. Which of the following holds good in all natural processes?
a) The Doppler Effect
b) Newton's law of gravitation
c) Electromagnetic law
d) Lenz's law

13. Which of the following leads to the law of conservation of energy?
a) Gravity
b) Isotropy
c) Nuclear force
d) Homogeneity of time

14. Which of the following leads to the law of conservation of angular momentum?

a) Isotropy of space

b) Homogeneity of time

c) Nuclear force

d) Gravity

15. Which of the following is the SI unit of luminous intensity?

a) Sterdian

b) Radian

c) Mole

d) Candela

16. Sterdian is the SI unit of which of the following?

a) Phase angle

b) Luminous intensity

c) Mass

d) Solid angle

17. How many light years are there in one metre?

a) 9.46×1015ly

b) 1.057×10-16ly

c) 1ly

d) 1×10-16ly

18. The radius of gold nucleus is 41.3fermi. Express its volume in m3.

a) 41.3×10-15 m3

b) 2.95×10-40 m3

c) 4.19 m3

d) 29.33 m3

19. Convert an acceleration of 2km/h2 into cm/s2.

a) 2×105 cm/s2

b) 0.0027 cm/s2

c) 0.0154 cm/s2

d) 0.055 cm/s2

## Applied Mechanics MCQ for Mechanical Engineering

1. Which of the following statement is true?

a) A scalar is any physical quantity that can be completely specified by its magnitude

b) A vector is any positive or negative physical quantity that can be completely specified by its magnitude

c) A scalar is any physical quantity that requires both a magnitude and a direction for its complete description

d) A scalar is any physical quantity that can be completely specified by its direction

2. For two vectors defined by an arrow with a head and a tail. The length of each vector and the angle between them represents:

a) Their magnitude's square and direction of the line of action respectively

b) Their magnitude and direction of the line of action respectively

c) Magnitude's square root and direction of the line of action respectively

d) Magnitude's square and the ratio of their lengths respectively

3. If a vector is multiplied by a scalar:

a) Then its magnitude is increased by the square root of that scalar's magnitude

b) Then its magnitude is increased by the square of that scalar's magnitude

c) Then its magnitude is increased by the amount of that scalar's magnitude

d) You cannot multiply the vector with a scalar

4. All the vectors quantities obey:

a) Parallelogram law of addition

b) Parallelogram law of multiplication

c) Parallelogram law of addition of square root of their magnitudes

d) Parallelogram law of addition of square of their magnitudes

5. A force vector with magnitude R and making an angle α with the x-axis is having its component along x-axis and y-axis as:

a) Rcosine (α) and Rsine(α)

b) Rcosine (180-α) and Rsine(α)

c) Rcosine (180-α) and Rsine(180+α)

d) Rcosine (α) and Rsine(180+α)

6. Dividing the X-axis component and the Y-axis component of the of the vector making an angle with Y-axis α will give us.

a) Cot α

b) Tan α

c) Sec α

d) 1

9. The magnitude of the resultant of the two vectors is always______________

a) Greater than one of the vector's magnitude

b) Smaller than one of the vector's magnitude

c) Depends on the angle between them

d) Axis we choose to calculate the magnitude

10. If two equal vector forces are mutually perpendicular then the resultant force is acting at which angle as compared to one of the vector?

a) 45 degree

b) 90 degree

c) 180 degree

d) 0 degree

11. What is the direction of the resultant vector if two vectors having equal length is placed in the Cartesian plane at the origin as, one being parallel to and heading towards positive x-axis and the other making 165 degree with it and heading in the opposite direction of that of the first one?

a) It is either in the 1$^{st}$ quadrant or in the 2$^{nd}$ quadrant

b) It is either in the 1$^{st}$ quadrant or in the 3$^{rd}$ quadrant

c) It is either in the 1$^{st}$ quadrant or in the 4$^{th}$ quadrant

d) Only in the 1$^{st}$ quadrant

12. Force vector R is having a______________

a) Length of R and a specific direction

b) Length of R

c) A specific direction

d) Length of magnitude equal to square root of R and a specific direction

13. In right handed coordinate system which axis is considered to be positive?

a) The thumb is z-axis, fingers curled from x-axis to y-axis

b) The thumb is x-axis, fingers curled from z-axis to y-axis

c) The thumb is y-axis, fingers curled from x-axis to z-axis

d) The thumb is z-axis, fingers curled from y-axis to x-axis

14. If A is any vector with Ai + Bj + Ck then what is the y-axis component of the vector?

a) B units

b) A units

c) C units

d) Square root of a sum of squares of the three, i.e. A, B and C

15. If the force vector F is having its x-axis component being equal to Z N, y-axis component be X N and z-axis component be Y N then vector F is best represented by?

a) Xi + Yj + Zk

b) Yi + Xj + Zk

c) Zi + Yj + Xk

d) Zi + Xj + Yk

16. Which statement is right for force vector F = Ai + Bj + Ck?

a) In rectangular components representation of any vector we have vector F = Ai + Bj + Ck

b) In rectangular components representation of any vector we have vector F = Ax + By + Cz

c) In rectangular components representation of any vector we have vector F = Fx + Fy + Fz

d) In rectangular components representation of any vector we have vector F = Fi + Fj + Fk

17. What is the magnitude of the Cartesian vector having the x, y and z axis components to be A, B and C?

a) Square root of the squares each A, B and C

b) Square of the squares each A, B and C

c) Cube root of the squares each A, B and C

d) Cube of the squares each A, B and C

18. What is $\cos\alpha$ for force vector F = Ax + By +Cz (Given $\alpha$, $\beta$ and $\gamma$ are the angles made by the vector with x, y and z axis respectively)?

a) B/F

b) C/F

c) A/F

d) 1

19. What is the sum of squares of the cosine angles made by the force vector with the coordinate axis?

a) 1

b) ½

c) 2

d) 3

20. What is the x-axis component of the force vector Ai + Bj +Ck with magnitude equal to F?

a) B

b) C

c) Fcosα

d) Fcosβ

21. For a vector F, Fcosβ is equal to zero. What does this refer?

a) X-axis component is zero

b) Y-axis component is zero

c) Z-axis component is zero

d) $\beta = 180^\circ$

22. Which statement is correct about the vector F?

a) F= Fcos β + Fcos α + Fcosγ

b) F= Fsin β + Fcos α + Fcosγ

c) F= Fcos β + Fsin α + Fcosγ

d) F= Fcos β + Fcos α + Fsinγ

23. Which is true?

a) ΣF = ΣFx + ΣFy + ΣFz

b) ΣF = -(ΣFx + ΣFy + ΣFz)

c) ΣF = ΣFxi + ΣFyj + ΣFzk

d) ΣF = -(ΣFxi+ ΣFyj + ΣFzk)

24. Find the angle α, for the vector making an angle by y and z axis as 60° and 45° respectively. It makes an angle of α with x-axis. The magnitude of the force is 200N.

a) 60°

b) 120°

c) 45°

d) 90°

**Civil Engineering Fundamentals for Mechanical Engineering**

1. Stones are obtained from rocks that are made up of:

a) Ores

b) Minerals

c) Chemical compounds

d) Crystals

2. Which one of the following is not a classification of stones?

a) Physical Classification

b) Mineralogical Classification

c) Chemical Classification

d) Practical Classification

3. The hot molten material occurring naturally below the surface of the Earth is called:

a) Lava
b) Slag
c) <u>Magma</u>
d) Tuff

4. At what depth and rate is a hypabyssal rock formed?
a) Slow cooling of magma at considerable depth
b) <u>Quick cooling of magma at a shallow depth</u>
c) Rapid cooling of magma at Earth's surface
d) Rapid cooling of magma at a shallow depth

5. What is a sedimentary deposit?
a) Weathered product remains at site
b) Weathered product carried away in solution
c) Weathered product gets carried away agents
d) <u>Insoluble weathered product is carried away in suspension</u>

6. Which factor disturbs the equilibrium of rocks, commencing metamorphism?
a) Increase in temperature
b) Decrease in temperature and pressure
c) <u>Increase in temperature and pressure</u>
d) Decrease in pressure

7. Which of the following is not a metamorphic change?
a) <u>Calcite to schist</u>
b) Limestone to marble
c) Shale to slate
d) Granite to gneisses

8. Which of the following rocks are hard and durable?
a) Argillaceous rocks
b) <u>Siliceous rocks</u>
c) Calcareous rocks
d) Carbonaceous rocks

9. Foliated structure is very common in case of:
a) Sedimentary rocks
b) Plutonic rocks
c) Igneous rocks
d) <u>Metamorphic rocks</u>

10. Granite is a type of:
a) <u>Plutonic rock</u>
b) Metamorphic rock

c) Hypabyssal rock
d) Volcanic rock

11. Which of the following is a good fire-resistant stone?
a) Clay
b) Granite
c) Quartz
d) Limestone

12. What is a freestone?
a) Stone free from impurities
b) Stone that doesn't require dressing
c) Metamorphic stone
d) Stone free from veins and planes of cleavage

13. Why are stones with lighter shades of colour preferred?
a) Easy to clean
b) Easily available
c) Don't spoil the appearance
d) Darker shades are heavier

14. Hardness is an important parameter considered in the construction of:
a) Slabs
b) Walls
c) Bridges
d) Arches

15. What is the required specific gravity for a good building stone?
a) Greater than 2.7
b) Less than 3
c) Greater than 3
d) Less than 2.7

16. The percentage absorption by weight of a good stone, after how many hours should not exceed .6?
a) 6 hrs
b) 12 hrs
c) 48 hrs
d) 24 hrs

17. What texture should a building stone possess?
a) Loose grains
b) Crystalline structure
c) Cavities

d) Cracks

18. Toughness index of a good stone should be more than:

a) 17

b) 18

c) 13

d) 19

**Manufacturing Technology for Mechanical Engineering**

1. Which of the following have a non-crystalline structure?

a) Iron

b) Quartz

c) Silica glass

d) Tungsten

2. Which of the following have a non-crystalline structure?

a) Steel

b) Nickel

c) High density polythene

d) Low density polythene

3. Which of the following is a characteristic of crystalline structure?

a) High density

b) Low density

c) Range of melting point

d) Varying structure

4. Which of the following is characteristic of non-crystalline structures?

a) Long range of periodicity

b) Well defined structure and geometry

c) Low density

d) Sharp diffraction pattern

5. Which of the following factor is not responsible for the formation of a non-crystalline structure?

a) Atomic packing has open structure

b) Primary bonds are absent

c) Formation of 1-dimensional chain molecule

d) Strong secondary bond

6. A cubic unit cell satisfies which of the following equations?

a) a=b=c, α=β=ϒ=90 degree

b) a≠b=c, α=β=ϒ=90 degree

c) a=b≠c, α=β=ϒ=90 degree

d) a=b=c, α≠β=ϒ=90 degree

7. A tetragon unit cell satisfies which of the following equations?
a) $a=b=c, \alpha=\beta=\Upsilon=90$ degree
b) $a\neq b=c, \alpha=\beta=\Upsilon=90$ degree
c) $a=b\neq c, \alpha=\beta=\Upsilon=90$ degree
d) $a=b=c, \alpha\neq\beta=\Upsilon=90$ degree
8. An Orthorhombic unit cell satisfies which of the following equations?
a) $a=b=c, \alpha=\beta=\Upsilon=90$ degree
b) $a\neq b\neq c, \alpha=\beta=\Upsilon=90$ degree
c) $a=b\neq c, \alpha=\beta=\Upsilon=90$ degree
d) $a=b=c, \alpha\neq\beta=\Upsilon=90$ degree
9. A Rhombohedra unit cell satisfies which of the following equations?
a) $a=b=c, \alpha=\beta=\Upsilon=90$ degree
b) $a\neq b=c, \alpha=\beta=\Upsilon=90$ degree
c) $a=b\neq c, \alpha=\beta=\Upsilon=90$ degree
d) $a=b=c, \alpha=\beta=\Upsilon\neq 90$ degree
10. A Hexagonal unit cell satisfies which of the following equations?
a) $a=b \neq c, \alpha=\beta=90$ degree, $\Upsilon=120$ degree
b) $a\neq b=c, \alpha=\beta=\Upsilon=90$ degree
c) $a=b\neq c, \alpha=\beta=\Upsilon=90$ degree
d) $a=b=c, \alpha\neq\beta=\Upsilon=90$ degree
11. A Monoclinic unit cell satisfies which of the following equations?
a) $a=b=c, \alpha=\beta=90$ degree $\neq \Upsilon$
b) $a\neq b=c, \alpha=\beta=\Upsilon=90$ degree
c) $a \neq b\neq c, \alpha=\beta=90$ degree $\neq \Upsilon$
d) $a=b=c, \alpha\neq\beta=\Upsilon=90$ degree
12. A Triclinic unit cell satisfies which of the following equations?
a) $a=b=c, \alpha=\beta=\Upsilon=90$ degree
b) $a\neq b=c, \alpha=\beta=\Upsilon=90$ degree
c) $a \neq b \neq c, \alpha \neq \beta \neq \Upsilon \neq 90$ degree
d) $a=b=c, \alpha\neq\beta=\Upsilon=90$ degree
13. Coordination number of simple cubic unit cell is equal to
a) 4
b) 6
c) 8
d) 2
14. Coordination number of face centered cubic unit cell is equal to
a) 4

b) 6
c) 8
d) 12
15. Coordination number of body centered cubic unit cell is equal to
a) 4
b) 6
c) 8
d) 2
16. Effective number of an atom in simple cubic unit cell is equal to
a) 4
b) 1
c) 8
d) 2
17. Effective number of an atom in face centered unit cell is equal to
a) 4
b) 1
c) 8
d) 2
18. Effective number of an atom in body centered cubic unit cell is equal to
a) 4
b) 1
c) 8
d) 2
19. Atomic Packing fraction in a percentage of simple cubic structure is given by
a) 74
b) 52
c) 68
d) 66
20. Atomic Packing fraction in a percentage of body centered structure is equal to
a) 74
b) 52
c) 68
d) 66
21. If radius of copper is 1.27 A°, then density of copper in Kg/m3 will be
a) 100.01

b) 86.25

c) 8979

d) 7968

22. Atomic Packing fraction in percentage of face centered cubic structure is equal to

a) 74

b) 52

c) 68

d) 66

**Fluid Mechanics MCQ for Mechanical Engineering**

1. Which one is in a state of failure?

a) Solid

b) Liquid

c) Gas

d) Fluid

2. A small shear force is applied on an element and then removed. If the element regains it's original position, what kind of an element can it be?

a) Solid

b) Liquid

c) Fluid

d) Gaseous

3. In which type of matter, one won't find a free surface?

a) Solid

b) Liquid

c) Gas

d) Fluid

4. If a person studies about a fluid which is at rest, what will you call his domain of study?

a) Fluid Mechanics

b) Fluid Statics

c) Fluid Kinematics

d) Fluid Dynamics

5. The value of the compressibility of an ideal fluid is

a) zero

b) unity

c) infinity

d) more than that of a real fluid

6. The value of the Bulk Modulus of an ideal fluid is

a) zero
b) unity
c) infinity
d) less than that of a real fluid

7. The value of the viscosity of an ideal fluid is
a) zero
b) unity
c) infinity
d) more than that of a real fluid

8. The value of the surface tension of an ideal fluid is
a) zero
b) unity
c) infinity
d) more than that of a real fluid

9. Which of the following statement is true about vapor pressure of a liquid?

a) Vapor pressure is closely related to molecular activity and temperature of the liquid

b) Vapor pressure is closely related to molecular activity but independent of the temperature of the liquid

c) Vapor pressure is not affected by molecular activity and temperature of the liquid

d) Vapor pressure is not affected by molecular activity and is independent of the temperature of the liquid

10. Which of the following equation correctly depicts the relation between the vapor pressure of a liquid and it's temperature?

a) Vapor pressure increases linearly with the increase in temperature of the liquid

b) Vapor pressure increases slightly with the increase in temperature of the liquid at low temperatures and the rate of increase goes high at higher temperatures

c) Vapor pressure increases rapidly with the increase in temperature of the liquid at low temperatures and the rate of increase goes low at higher temperatures

d) Vapor pressure remains unchanged with the increase in temperature of the liquid

11. Which of the following is the condition for the boiling of a liquid?

a) Absolute pressure of a liquid must be greater than or equal to it's vapor pressure

b) Absolute pressure of a liquid must be less than or equal to it's vapor pressure

c) Absolute pressure of a liquid must be equal to it's vapor pressure

d) Absolute pressure of a liquid must be greater than it's vapor pressure

12. Which of the following machines have the possibility of cavitation?

a) Reaction turbines and centrifugal pumps

b) Reaction turbines and reciprocating pumps

c) Impulse turbines and centrifugal pumps

d) Impulse turbines and reciprocating pumps

13. The three liquids 1, 2, and 3 with vapor pressures V1, V2 and V3 respectively, are kept under same pressure. If $V1 > V2 > V3$, which liquid will start boiling early?

a) liquid 1

b) liquid 2

c) liquid 3

d) they will start boiling at the same time

14. Equal amount of a particular liquid is poured into three similar containers, namely 1, 2 and 3, at a temperature of T1, T2 and T3 respectively. If $T1 < T2 < T3$, the liquid in which container will have the highest vapor pressure?

a) container 1

b) container 2

c) container 3

d) the vapor pressure of the liquid will remain the same irrespective of it's temperature

15. The absolute pressure of a water is 0.5kN above it's vapor pressure. If it flows with a velocity of 1m/s, what will be the value of Cavitation Number describing the flow induced boiling?

a) 0.25

b) 0.5

c) 1

d) 2

16. Which of the following is correct regarding the formation and collapse of vapor bubbles in a liquid?

a) Vapor bubbles are formed when the fluid pressure goes above the vapor pressure and collapses when the fluid pressure goes above the bubble pressure

b) Vapor bubbles are formed when the fluid pressure goes above the vapor pressure and collapses when the fluid pressure goes below the bubble pressure

c) Vapor bubbles are formed when the fluid pressure drops below the vapor pressure and collapses when the fluid pressure goes below the bubble pressure

d) Vapor bubbles are formed when the fluid pressure drops below the vapor pressure and collapses when the fluid pressure goes above the bubble pressure

**Thermodynamics MCQ for Mechanical Engineering**

1. A piston/cylinder with a cross-sectional area of 0.01 m^2 is resting on the stops. With an outside pressure of 100 kPa, what should be the water pressure to lift the piston?

a) 178kPa

b) 188kPa

c) 198kPa

d) 208kPa

3. A large exhaust fan in a lab room keeps the pressure inside at 10 cm water relative vacuum to the hallway? What is the net force acting on the door measuring 1.9 m by 1.1 m?

a) 2020 N

b) 2030 N

c) 2040 N

d) 2050 N

4. A 5 m long vertical tube having cross sectional area 200 cm^2 is placed in a water. It is filled with 15°C water, with the bottom closed and the top open to 100 kPa atmosphere. How much water is present in tube?

a) 99.9 kg

b) 109.9 kg

c) 89.9 kg

d) 79.9 kg

5. A 5 m long vertical tube having cross sectional area 200 cm2 is placed in a water. It is filled with 15°C water, with the bottom closed and the top open to 100 kPa atmosphere. What is the pressure at the bottom of tube ?

a) 119 kPa

b) 129 kPa

c) 139 kPa

d) 149 kPa

6. Find the pressure of water at 200°C and having specific volume of 1.5 m3/kg.

a) 0.9578 m3/kg
b) 0.8578 m3/kg
c) 0.7578 m3/kg
d) 0.6578 m3/kg

7. Find the pressure of water at 200°C and having specific volume of 1.5 m^3/kg.

a) 141.6 kPa
b) 111.6 kPa
c) 121.6 kPa
d) 161.6 kPa

8. A 5m^3 container is filled with 840 kg of granite (density is 2400 kg/m^3) and the rest of the volume is air (density is 1.15 kg/m^3). Find the mass of air present in the container.

a) 9.3475 kg
b) 8.3475 kg
c) 6.3475 kg
d) 5.3475 kg

9. A 100 m tall building receives superheated steam at 200 kPa at ground and leaves saturated vapour from the top at 125 kPa by losing 110 kJ/kg of heat. What should be the minimum inlet temperature at the ground of the building so that no steam will condense inside the pipe at steady state?

a) 363.54°C
b) 263.54°C
c) 163.54°C
d) none of the mentioned

10. The pressure gauge on an air tank shows 60 kPa when the diver is 8 m down in the ocean. At what depth will the gauge pressure be zero?

a) 34.118 m
b) 24.118 m
c) 14.118 m
d) none of the mentioned

11. A piston-cylinder device initially contains air at 150 kPa and 27°C. At this state, the volume is 400 litre. The mass of the piston is such that a 350 kPa pressure is required to move it. The air is now heated until its volume has doubled. Determine the final temperature.

a) 1400 K
b) 400 K
c) 500 K
d) 1500 K

12. A piston-cylinder device initially contains air at 150 kPa and 27°C. At this state, the volume is 400 litre. The mass of the piston is such that a 350 kPa pressure is required to move it. The air is now heated until its volume has doubled. Determine work done by the air.

a) 120 kJ
b) 130 kJ
c) 100 kJ
d) 140 kJ

13. Find the change in u for carbon dioxide between 600 K and 1200 K for a constant Cv0 value.

a) 291.8 kJ/kg
b) 391.8 kJ/kg
c) 491.8 kJ/kg
d) 591.8 kJ/kg

14. Calculate the change in enthalpy of carbon dioxide from 30 to 1500°C at 100 kPa at constant specific heat.

a) 2237.7 kJ/kg
b) 1637.7 kJ/kg
c) 1237.7 kJ/kg
d) 2337.7 kJ/kg

15. A sealed rigid vessel has volume of 1 m3 and contains 2 kg of water at 100°C. The vessel is now heated. If a safety pressure valve is installed, at what pressure should the valve be set to have a maximum temperature of 200°C ?

a) 431.3 kPa
b) 531.3 kPa
c) 631.3 kPa
d) 731.3 kPa

16. A system undergoing change in state from A to B along path 'X' receives 100 J heat and does 40 J work. It returns to state A from B along path 'Y' with work input of 30 J. Calculate the heat transfer involved along the path 'Y'.

a) – 60 J
b) 60 J

c) <u>– 90 J</u>
d) 90 J
17. Which of the following were used as fixed points before 1954?
a) The ice point
b) The steam point
c) <u>All of the mentioned</u>
d) None of the mentioned
18. What is the standard fixed point of thermometry?
a) The ice point
b) The steam point
c) <u>The triple point of water</u>
d) None of the mentioned
19. All gases and vapours approach ideal gas behaviour at?
a) High pressure and high density
b) <u>Low pressure and low density</u>
c) High pressure and low density
d) Low pressure and high density
20. The value of ratio of the steam point temperature to the ice point temperature is?
a) 1.466
b) 1.266
c) 1.166
d) <u>1.366</u>
21. Celsius temperature of the triple point of water is ( in degree Celsius)?
a) -0.00
b) 0.00
c) <u>0.01</u>
d) None of the mentioned
22. Which of the following is chosen as the standard thermometric substance?
a) <u>Gas</u>
b) Liquid
c) Solid
d) All of the mentioned
23. A real gas behaves as an ideal gas when?
a) Temperature approaches zero
b) <u>Pressure approaches zero</u>

c) Both temperature and pressure approaches zero

d) None of the mentioned

24. The temperature interval from the oxygen point to the gold point is divided into how many parts?

a) 2

b) 3

c) 4

d) 1

**Strength of Material MCQ for Mechanical Engineering**

1. What is tensile stress?

a) The ratio of change in length to the original length

b) The ratio of original length to the change in length

c) The ratio of tensile force to the change in length

d) The ratio of change in length to the tensile force applied

2. Find the strain of a brass rod of length 250mm which is subjected to a tensile load of 50kN when the extension of rod is equal to 0.3mm?

a) 0.025

b) 0.0012

c) 0.0046

d) 0.0014

3. Find the elongation of an steel rod of 100mm length when it is subjected to a tensile strain of 0.005?

a) 0.2mm

b) 0.3mm

c) 0.5mm

d) 0.1mm

4. A tensile test was conducted on a mild steel bar. The diameter and the gauge length of bat was 3cm and 20cm respectively. The extension was 0.21mm. What is the value to strain ?

a) 0.0010

b) 0.00105

c) 0.0105

d) 0.005

5. q. Strain is a fundamental behaviour of material.

r. Strain does not have a unit.

a) Both q. and r. are true and r. is the correct explanation of q

b) Both q. and r. ate true but r. is not the correct explanatio of q

c) q. is true but r. is false

d) r. is true but q. is false

6. A tensile test was conducted on a steel bar. The gauge length of the bar was 10cm and the extension was 2mm. What will be the percentage elongation ?

a) 0.002

b) 0.02

c) 0.2

d) 2

7. The lateral strain is ?

a) The ratio of axial deformation to the original length

b) The ratio of deformation in area to the original area

c) The strain at right angles to the direction of applied load

d) The ratio of length of body to the tensile force applied on it

8. The unit of force in S.I. units is ?

a) Kilogram

b) Newton

c) Watt

d) Dyne

9. Which of the following is not the unit of distance?

a) Angstrom

b) Light year

c) Micron

d) Milestone

10. A solid cube is subjected to equal normal forces on all its faces. The volumetric strain will be x-times the linear strain in any of the three axes when ?

a) X=1

b) X=2

c) X=3

d) X=4

11. A rod 200cm long is subjected to an axial pull due to which it elongates about 2mm. Calculate the amount of strain?

a) 0.001

b) 0.01

c) 0.02

d) 0.002

12. Some structural members subjected to long time sustained loads deform progressively with time especially at elevated temperatures. What

is such a phenomenon called?

a) Fatigue

b) Creep

c) Creep relaxation

d) Fracture

13. Find the strain of a brass rod of length 100mm which is subjected to a tensile load of 50kN when the extension of rod is equal to 0.1mm?

a) 0.01

b) 0.001

c) 0.05

d) 0.005

14. In the given figure a stepped column carries loads. What will be the maximum normal stress in the column at B in the larger diameter column if the ratio of P/A here is unity?

a) 1/1.5

b) 1

c) 2/1.5

d) 2

15. The stress which acts in a direction perpendicular to the area is called

a) shear stress

b) Normal stress

c) Thermal stress

d) None of the mentioned

16. Which of these are types of normal stresses?

a) Tensile and compressive stresses

b) Tensile and thermal stresses

c) Shear and bending

d) Compressive and plane stresses

17. In a body loaded under plane stress conditions, what is the number of independent stress components ?

a) 1

b) 2

c) 3

d) 6

18. If a bar of large length when held vertically and subjected to a load at its lower end, its won-weight produces additional stress. The maximum stress will be

a) At the lower cross-section

b) At the built-in upper cross-section

c) At the central cross-section

d) At every point of the bar

19. Which type of stress does in a reinforcement bar is taken by the concrete ?

a) Tensile stress

b) Compressive stress

c) Shear stress

d) Bending stress

20. A material has Poisson's ratio of 0.5. If uniform pressure of 300GPa is applied to that material , What will be the volumetric strain of it?

a) 0.50

b) 0.20

c) 0.25

d) Zero

21. A diagram which shows the variations of the axial load for all sections of the pan of a beam, is called

a) Bending moment diagram

b) Shear force diagram

c) Thrust diagram

d) Stress diagram

22. The stress induced in a body, when subjected to two equal and opposite forces which are acting tangentially across the resisting section resulting the shearing of the body across its section is called

a) Bending stress

b) Compressive stress

c) Shear strain

d) Shear stress

23. What is the formula for shear stress?

a) Shear resistance / shear area

b) Force / unit area

c) Bending strain / area

d) Shear stress / length

24. Which of the following stresses are associated with the tightening of nut on a bolt?

P. Crushing and shear stress in threads

Q. Bending stress due to the bending of bolt

R. Torsional shear stress due to frictional resistance between the nut and the bolt

Select the correct answer using the codes given below

a) P and Q

b) P and R

c) Only P

d) Only R

25. The transverse shear stress acting in a beam of rectangular cross-section, subjected to a transverse shear load, is

a) variable with maximum at the bottom of the beam

b) Variable with maximum at the top of the beam

c) Uniform

d) Variable with maximum on the neutral axis

26. A block 100mm x 100mm base and 10mm height. What will the direct shear stress in the element when a tangential force of 10kN is applied to the upper edge to a displacement 1mm relative to lower face?

a) 1Pa

b) 1MPa

c) 10MPa

d) 100Pa

**Power Plant MCQ for Mechanical Engineering**

1. Which of these is a 'fissile fuel'?

a) Thorium

b) Carbon

c) Potassium

d) Graphite

2. Which of these is a 'working fluid' in liquid phase?

a) Water

b) Steam

c) Mercury

d) Oxygen

3. Which of these is an output of a 'Furnace'?

a) Fuel gas

b) Air

c) Flue gases

d) Water Vapor

4. What kind of energy output is obtained from a 'Steam Power Plant'?

a) Heat energy

b) Sound energy
c) Electricity
d) Thermal energy
5. What kind of a process does a 'Steam Power Plant' undergoes?
a) Adiabatic
b) Cyclic
c) Irreversible
d) Expansion
6. Water that is fed back to the boiler by the pump is called?
a) Adsorbate
b) Absorbate
c) Condenset
d) Condensate
7. The net change in internal energy in a steam power plant is?
a) Positive
b) Negative
c) Zero
d) None of the mentioned
8. The product of efficiency & heat transferred to the working fluid is?
a) Net temperature change
b) Net work done
c) Net enthalpy change
d) None of the mentioned
9. The components of a Steam Power Plant are?
a) Evaporator, Condenser, Boiler, Expansion valve
b) Evaporator, Condenser, Boiler, Turbine
c) Boiler, Turbine, Condenser, Pump
d) Boiler, Turbine, Pump, Expansion valve
10. Shaft work is fed to ___________ for getting an electrical output.
a) Motor
b) Generator
c) Rotor
d) Accelerator
11. Ideal 'Rankine Cycle' is a ___________ process.
a) Reversible
b) Irreversible
c) Both of the mentioned
d) None of the mentioned

12. For analytical purposes, the Rankine Cycle is assumed to be in?
a) Unsteady flow operation
b) Turbulent flow operation
c) Steady flow operation
d) Laminar flow operation
13. The net work done in a Rankine Cycle is the difference of?
a) Condenser work & Boiler work
b) Boiler work & Pump work
c) Turbine Work & Pump work
d) Condenser work & Pump work
14. In a Rankine Cycle, heat input is provided to?
a) Condenser
b) Pump
c) Turbine
d) Boiler
15. In a Rankine Cycle, heat output is obtained from?
a) Condenser
b) Boiler
c) Turbine
d) Pump
16. The water that flows from the Pump is?
a) Compressible
b) Incompressible
c) Unsteady
d) None of the mentioned
17. Steam Rate is the reciprocal of __________
a) Net work done
b) Heat extracted from condenser
c) Heat given to reciprocal
d) Work done by turbine.
18. Which of these is sometimes neglected?
a) Turbine work
b) Pump work
c) Condenser heat
d) Boiler heat
19. Efficiency of a Rankine Cycle is also expressed as___________
a) Capacity Ratio
b) Heat Rate

c) Heat Ratio

d) Steam Rate

20. Steam Power Plants are more popular in electric power generation because

a) Work output of turbine is very large than work input to the pump

b) Work output of turbine is very small than work input to the pump

c) Work output of turbine is equal to work input to the pump

d) None of the mentioned.

21. The most common type of Evaporator is?

a) Flooded Evaporator

b) Plate Evaporator

c) Coil Evaporator

d) Brine Evaporator

22. In Rankine Cycle, water is converted to saturated liquid in ______________

a) Evaporator

b) Economizer

c) Superheater

d) Preheater

23. Phase change at constant pressure takes place in?

a) Economiser

b) Evaporator

c) Superheater

d) Air-Preheater

24. Which of these factors don't cause Internal Irreversibility of a Rankine cycle?

a) Throttling

b) Mixing

c) Fluid Friction

d) Fluid flow

CHAPTER FOURTEEN

# Mechanical Engineering Basic Computer Skills MCQ

1] WWW stands for ?

A] World Whole Web

B] Wide World Web

C] Web World Wide

D] World Wide Web

2] Which of the following are components of Central Processing Unit (CPU) ?

A] Arithmetic logic unit, Mouse

B] Arithmetic logic unit, Control unit

C] Arithmetic logic unit, Integrated Circuits

D] Control Unit, Monitor

3] Which among following first generation of computers had ?

A] Vaccum Tubes and Magnetic Drum

B] Integrated Circuits

C] Magnetic Tape and Transistors

D] All of above

4] Where is RAM located ?

A] Expansion Board

B] External Drive

C] Mother Board

D] All of above

5] If a computer has more than one processor then it is known as ?

A] Uniprocess

B] Multiprocessor

C] Multithreaded

D] Multiprogramming

6] If a computer provides database services to other, then it will be known as ?

A] Web server

B] Application server

C] Database server

D] FTP server

7] Full form of URL is ?

A] Uniform Resource Locator

B] Uniform Resource Link

C] Uniform Registered Link

D] Unified Resource Link

8] In which of the following form, data is stored in computer ?

A] Decimal

B] Binary

C] HexaDecimal

D] Octal

9] Technology used to provide internet by transmitting data over wires of telephone network is ?

A] Transmitter

B] Diodes

C] HHL

D] DSL

10] Which level language is Assembly Language ?

A] high-level programming language

B] medium-level programming language

C] low-level programming language

D] machine language

11] Documents, Movies, Images and Photographs etc are stored at a ?

A] Application Sever

B] Web Sever

C] Print Server

D] File Server

12] Which of following is used in RAM ?

A] Conductor

B] Semi Conductor

C] Vaccum Tubes

D] Transistor

13] What is full form of GUI in terms of computers ?

A] Graphical user Instrument
B] Graphical unified Interface
C] Graphical unified Instrument
D] Graphical user Interface
14] What is full form of ALU ?
A] Arithmetic logic unit
B] Allowed logic unit
C] Ascii logic unit
D] Arithmetic least unit
15] Who was the Founder of Bluetooth ?
A] Ericson
B] Martin Cooper
C] Steve Jobs
D] Apple
16] Who was the father of Internet ?
A] Chares Babbage
B] Vint Cerf
C] Denis Riche
D] Martin Cooper
17] Verification is process of ?
A] Access
B] Login
C] Logout
D] Authentication
18] What is LINUX ?
A] Malware
B] Operating System
C] Application Program
D] Firmware
19] What is the name of first super computer of India ?
A] Saga 220
B] PARAM 8000
C] ENIAC
D] PARAM 6000
20] Which is most common language used in web designing ?
A] C
B] C++
C] PHP

D] HTML

21] Who is also known as Father of Computer ?

A] Vint Cerf

B] Tim Berner Lee

C] Charles Babbage

D] Steve Jobs

CHAPTER FIFTEEN

# Mechanical Engineering Sheet Metal Work MCQ

1] Which method of development is used for developing a rectangular tray?

A] triangular method

B] radial line method

C] parallel line method

D] trial and error method

2] What is the profile of the knife cutting edge of the upper blade of the hand level shear?

A] curved

B] straight

C] inclined

D] beveled

3] For what purpose a groover is used in sheet metal work?

A] to make a hem

B] to make grooves

C] to close and lock the seams

D] to strength then the edge of a job

4] Which type of stake is to be selected for making sharp bends, folding of edges of sheet metal?

A] hatchet stake

B] beak iron stake

C] square edge stake

D] tinman's anvil stake

5] Ammonium chloride is used as a flux for soldering...

A] steel

B] aluminium

C] galvanized iron

D] stainless steel

6] Name the tool used to make and finish the leak proof joints of a pipe T joint

A] groover

B] setting hammer

C] creasing hammer

D] round bottom stake

7] Which one of the following metals will not permit X-rays to pass through?

A] stainless steel

B] aluminium

C] lead

D] tin

8] The frequency of up and down vibration of the cutting edge in a nibbling machine is...

A] 1000 to 1500 times

B] 1500 to 2500 times

C] 2800 to 3000 times

D] 3000 to 3500 times

9] Name the instrument used to check the perpendicularity of the branch pipe with the main pipe of a pipe T joint

A] protractor

B] try square

C] spirit level

D] straight edge

10].Which type of notch is used when a single hem meets at right angles?

A] V notch

B] slit notch

C] slant notch

D] square notch

11] To cut out small apertures which punch and die type of machine is used?

A] shear type nibbler

B] punch type nibbler

C] circular cutting machine

D] guillotine shearing machine

12] The overheating of the blow pipe nozzle is to be avoided because it will

A] cause back fire

B] consume more oxygen and acetylene

C] create burn through defect in the joint

D] create undercut defect in the joint

13] State the nozzle size you will select to weld a 3.15mm thick mild steel sheet

A] 3

B.5

C] 7

D] 10

14] The type of flame to be set for welding brass is...

A] air acetylene flame

B] neutral flame

C] oxidizing flame

D] carburizing flame

15] What is the maximum thickness of mild steel sheet recommended for gas welding using leftward technique?

A] 12mm

B] 10mm

C] 8mm

D] 5mm

16].The distance between the root and toe of a fillet weld is called...

A] root gap

B] leg length

C] reinforcement

D] throat thickness

17] Name the weld defect which occurs due to improper cleaning of the mild steel sheet edge and surface

A] lack of root penetration

B] burn through

C] undercut

D] porosity

18] Which of the following mechanical properties of metals gives resistance to pulling forces?

A] toughness

B] ductility

C] hardness

D] tensile strength

www.ingramcontent.com/pod-product-compliance
Ingram Content Group UK Ltd.
Pitfield, Milton Keynes, MK11 3LW, UK
UKHW021906190726
13853UKWH00002B/531